THE YORKSHIRE TERRIER

Deborah Wood

The Yorkshire Terrier

Project Team
Editor: Stephanie Hays
Copy Editor: Joann Woy
Indexer: Ann W. Truesdale
Design: Lundquist Design and Angela Stanford
Series Design: Mada Design
Series Originator: Dominique De Vito

T.F.H. Publications
President/CEO: Glen S. Axelrod
Executive Vice President: Mark E. Johnson
Publisher: Christopher T. Reggio
Production Manager: Kathy Bontz

T.F.H. Publications, Inc.
One TFH Plaza
Third and Union Avenues
Neptune City, NJ 07753

ISBN 978-0-7938-3644-4
08 09 10 11 12   5 7 9 10 8 6

Library of Congress Cataloging-in-Publication Data
Wood, Deborah, 1952-
  The Yorkshire terrier / Deborah Wood.
       p. cm.
  Includes index.
  ISBN 0-7938-3644-1 (alk. paper)
  1. Yorkshire terrier. I. Title.
  SF429.Y6W66 2005
  636.76—dc22

This book has been published with the intent to provide accurate and authoritative information in regard to the subject matter within. While every reasonable precaution has been taken in preparation of this book, the author and publisher expressly disclaim responsibility for any errors, omissions, or adverse effects arising from the use or application of the information contained herein. The techniques and suggestions are used at the reader's discretion and are not to be considered a substitute for veterinary care. If you suspect a medical problem consult your veterinarian.

The Leader In Responsible Animal Care For Over 50 Years!®
www.tfh.com

TABLE OF CONTENTS

HISTORY

of the Yorkshire Terrier

f you like to wear pearls with your jeans, you're a little bit like a Yorkshire Terrier. If you go country dancing in your tuxedo, you might share the soul of a Yorkie.

On the outside, Yorkies are all elegance. You'll frequently see them at dog shows, gliding to Best in Show, their red ribbons sparkling and their long coats trailing behind them. But underneath that refined exterior is a game little dog whose ancestors were blue-collar ratting dogs in industrial England.

If you understand the history of your little dog, you'll understand much of what makes the Yorkshire Terrier a unique, charming, and entertaining pet. Thanks to that history, these small dogs are a little bit city and a little bit country, a little bit gritty and a little bit suave.

FROM SCOTLAND TO ENGLAND: GAME TERRIERS AND THE SCOTS WORKING CLASS

For hundreds of years, Scots working-class people were accompanied by their terriers. The wealthy elite owned almost all the land, and only people of prosperity and high social standing were allowed to own large hunting dogs. Because rich land owners were afraid that the working class would poach on their property, poor people in Scotland were only allowed to have small dogs. The game little dogs whom these people developed hunted all kinds of creatures, including rats, rabbits, squirrels, otters, badgers, and foxes. Life wasn't easy for these impoverished humans or their dogs. It required grit just to survive.

Yorkshire Terriers were originally bred for their hunting ability, not for their physical appearance.

Pound for pound, no dogs on Earth are as tough or as plucky as the terriers developed by the Scots working class. Imagine the courage it took to follow a 40-pound (18.1 kg) badger with punishing claws and teeth into its den, or to take on 100 rats!

Migrating to England

When the Industrial Revolution changed the face of the world, many Scots came to Yorkshire county in northern England in the 1800s to work in the mills and the mines. Yorkshire was a rough terrain, and the cities of the time were little better, with harsh working conditions. Many of the Scots came to the northern England city of Yorkshire to work as weavers in the textile mills. They brought with them their little dogs, who hunted the rats in the factories and became house pets.

We'll never know the exact mix of dogs that created the early Yorkshire Terriers, because these hard-working, blue-collar dog lovers weren't keeping the meticulous breeding records that people keep today. The breeding knowledge of these early Yorkie fanciers came from surviving a hard life, not from books. In fact, they were not breeding necessarily for size, color, or a specific appearance;

they were breeding for dogs who were good game ratters—tough little dogs who could keep the city vermin at bay. These ancestors of today's Yorkies certainly earned their keep.

Inevitably, cross breeding occurred between the dogs the Scots brought to Yorkshire and the local English dogs. The Waterside Terrier, a small, longish-coated, bluish-gray dog, is said to be an ancestor of the Yorkshire Terrier. The Waterside Terrier in turn was formed by the crossing of the old rough-coated black-and-tan English Terrier and the Paisley and Clydesdale Terriers—long-bodied dogs with somewhat silky coats. Quite a bit of speculation also suggests that, in the later part of the 1800s, Maltese were introduced to the line to make the Yorkshire Terrier's coat more silky.

Whatever the exact intermingling may have been, by the mid-1800s, a breed that was unique to Yorkshire county emerged: a small, game terrier with long, relatively silky hair. These dogs lived with their families, followed them to work in the mills and mines, and on weekends, provided diversion. At the time, as awful as it may seem today, it was popular to bet on all kinds of animal fights, including fights between bears and dogs and bulls and dogs. Ratting competitions were held, in which terriers were thrown in with rats, and the dog who killed the most rats in a given time won. The Yorkshire Terrier's ancestors were among the best of the ratting dogs. In fact, when your little Yorkie pounces on his favorite toy and shakes it, he's mimicking the motion that helped his ancestors kill rats.

The Yorkshire Terriers of mid-nineteenth century England

Best in Show: Famous Yorkies in the Ring

Yorkshire Terriers have made it to the pinnacle of dogdom in both the United States and England.

In 1978, a Yorkie named Ch. Cede Higgins got the nod for Best in Show at the Westminster Kennel Club Dog Show in New York's Madison Square Garden. The final competition happened to be held on Valentine's Day that year. Handler Marlene Lutovsky wore a red dress, and of course, the dog wore a red bow (although in a nod to fashion, Higgins' bow had white polka dots). When Ann Rodgers Clark, one of the most famous dog show judges of all time, gave Best in Show to Higgins, she said, "He has to be the best Yorkie I've ever seen, and he showed his heart out."

Show Yorkies like Higgins take a lot of work, even though this little guy weighed in at just 5 pounds (2.3 kg). After the win, Higgins' handler admitted she had to get up every morning at 5 o'clock to brush the dog's teeth; comb out, condition, and put his coat in show "wraps"; and put clean booties on his feet so that he wouldn't scratch or muss his hair.

Only one feat in the world of show dogs matches winning Best in Show at Westminster, and that's winning Crufts. This English equivalent to Westminster boasts about 20,000 entries every year, and about 100,000 fans come out to see the dogs. In 1997, Ch. Ozmilion Mystification went into Crufts as the favorite, because he was the top-winning dog of all breeds in England in 1996. He left the ring the ultimate winner, having been crowned Best in Show.

The AKC and KC

The American Kennel Club (AKC), founded in 1884, is the most influential dog club in the United States. The AKC is a "club of clubs," meaning that its members are other kennel clubs, not individual people. The AKC registers purebred dogs, supervises dog shows, and is concerned with all dog-related matters, including public education and legislation. It collects and publishes the official standards for all of its recognized breeds.

The United Kingdom version of the AKC is called the Kennel Club. However, the Kennel Club's members are individual persons. The membership of the Kennel Club is restricted to a maximum of 1,500 UK members in addition to 50 overseas members and a small number of honorary life members. The Kennel Club promotes responsible dog ownership and works on important issues like canine health and welfare.

weren't quite the same as the Yorkies of today. Generally, they were larger, weighing approximately 12 pounds (5.4 kg). Their coats were silky compared to other terriers, but they still were coarser than contemporary dogs. Mid-nineteenth century Yorkies had coats that were of medium rather than floor length. Still, they were distinct from other terriers of the time, and you definitely can see the family resemblance in the Yorkies of today.

Dog shows became something of an obsession in Victorian England.

Dog Shows and the Father of the Breed

The world of dogs in general and the Yorkshire Terrier in particular changed in 1859, when the first dog show was held in Newcastle-on-Tyne, England. Just as dog shows have recently become wildly popular in the United States, they became something of an obsession in Victorian England. In fact, Queen Victoria herself was quite a dog lover, and dogs who belonged to her were shown in both England and the United States. Yorkies were first shown at a dog show in 1861, and almost immediately great interest was expressed in these charismatic little dogs.

One of the stars of the early show scene was a dog named Huddersfield Ben. He was born in 1865 and died when he was run over by a carriage in 1871. However, during his short years on this earth, he was both a popular show dog and a popular sire. He won 74 awards at dog shows and also was very successful in ratting competitions.

Ben looked different from modern-day Yorkies. A painting of this famous dog shows a long body, face, and muzzle, capped with a large nose. His coat was cut shorter than today's Yorkies, but that may be because he worked as a ratter. Still, despite these differences, you can see the beginnings of the breed in this handsome dog.

Huddersfield Ben passed on his traits to his offspring and to their offspring. He also was one of the first sires to have offspring who consistently weighed less than 5 pounds (2.3 kg), which set the breed type for future generations. When Ben died, he was stuffed

Yorkie Doodle Dandie

One of World War II's most famous dog heroes was a 4-pound (1.8 kg) Yorkie named Smokey. Somehow, this little dog ended up alone, shivering in a foxhole on the island of New Guinea during some of the war's bloodiest fighting. She was adopted by Bill Wynne, a U.S. Army aerial photographer.

Smokey became something of a mascot, visiting hospitals and cheering up wounded soldiers. One day, though, the Army needed her intelligence and natural terrier instincts to save the day. The Army wanted to thread telephone wires through a 70-foot-long (21.3 m) section of 8-inch (20.3 cm) pipe. Little Smokey was called on to pull a string through the long pipe, which she successfully accomplished. The Army was later able to fasten the heavier telephone lines to the string, and communications were set up. Little Smokey was a hero!

Happily, Wynne brought Smokey home at the end of the war and wrote a book called Yorkie Doodle Dandie to tell her story. Wynne is now retired and living in Cleveland. As of this writing, plans are underway to honor Smokey with a statue in the Veterans Memorial section of a major Cleveland park. Unlike other bronze statues that make figures larger than life, Smokey will be shown life-sized, curled up in a helmet. The statue will demonstrate just how much one little dog was able to accomplish.

and preserved for years for people to see. If you were to trace your Yorkie's pedigree back far enough, you almost certainly would find Huddersfield Ben on the pedigree.

It must be said that early English dog shows lumped a lot of fairly dissimilar dogs together in broad categories. Originally, the dogs who are now called Yorkshire Terriers were shown under the name "Broken-Haired Scotch Terrier." In 1870, though, a writer by the name of Angus Sutherland reported in The Field magazine after a dog show in Westmoreland, England, that "[the dogs] ought no longer be called Scotch Terriers, but Yorkshire Terriers for having been so improved there." The fanciers agreed, and the name was changed. In fact, Yorkshire Terriers competed in a separate breed category at English dog shows after 1870. Soon, these charming little dogs, who were popular at dog shows, caught the public's attention, and Yorkies subsequently became fashionable pets. Just as young women love to carry around their Yorkies today, the breed became popular parlor pets in England. At the same time, show enthusiasts bred increasingly for silky coats and smaller size.

Registration of the Yorkshire Terrier in England

By the 1870s, it was clear that an organization was needed to regulate the registration and showing of dogs. In April of 1873, a group of 12 English "gentlemen" dog enthusiasts founded the Kennel Club. The Kennel Club started keeping the official pedigrees of purebred dogs in England and maintaining show records. This organization approved breed standards and accepted dog breeds for registration. The Kennel Club recognized Yorkshire Terriers as a separate breed in 1886.

Although the Yorkshire Terrier has been a favorite in England for many years, in 2004, for the first time in decades, the breed dropped out of the top ten most registered breeds.

THE YORKSHIRE TERRIER IN THE UNITED STATES

Sometime around 1870, the first Yorkies were imported to the United States, and the first reported litter was born in 1872. These spirited little dogs soon became popular with American dog show devotees.

Until World War II ended, Yorkies mostly were a favorite of serious dog show enthusiasts, with less than 200 Yorkies registered

The Yorkshire Terrier immediately become a popular dog show contender upon arriving in the US in the 1870s.

The modern Yorkie can excel as both a show dog and a loving family pet.

with the American Kennel Club (AKC) in a typical year. In the 1950s, the breed began to experience the beginnings of its surge to popularity in America, with about 1,000 dogs registered in 1960.

Then, Hollywood found the glamorous Yorkie. Audrey Hepburn always was pictured with her canine version of "arm candy," named Mr. Famous. In the television show *Green Acres* (which ran from 1965 to 1971), Eva Gabor's socialite character carried her faithful Yorkie, dubbed Mignon. In real life, Eva had a Yorkie named Baby. Even President Richard Nixon got into the act, with a White House pet Yorkie named Pasha.

Over the years, Yorkie popularity has continued to soar, with more than 13,000 registered in 1970, nearly 25,000 registered in 1980 and almost 45,000 registered in 2004.

Dog Shows in the United States

As mentioned earlier, the popularity of dog shows eventually

spread to America, and Yorkies were part of that popularity. As early as 1878, in American dog shows, Yorkshire Terriers were shown in two classes: one for dogs weighing up to 5 pounds (2.3 kg), and the other for dogs weighing more than 5 pounds (2.3 kg). Thirty-three Yorkshire Terriers were entered in the Westminster Kennel Club dog show in 1878—13 dogs in the up to 5-pound (2.3 kg) class and 18 in the over 5-pound (2.3 kg) competition. Although the breed was larger overall then than it is now, certainly many Yorkies who maintained the same size as today's small show dogs.

The first champion in the United States was a dog named Bradford Henry. Not surprisingly, he was a descendent of Huddersfield Ben.

Registration of the Yorkshire Terrier in the United States

The American Kennel Club was formed in 1884, and it admitted Yorkshire Terriers for registration in 1885. The first Yorkie registered was a dog named Belle.

Today, Yorkies continue to ride a wave of enormous popularity in the United States. In fact, in 2004, Yorkshire Terriers ranked as the fifth most popular breed registered with the AKC, with 43,522 dogs (up from 2003, when the breed ranked sixth, with 38,246 registrations). Only Labrador Retrievers, Golden Retrievers, German Shepherd Dogs, and Beagles outranked Yorkies.

Yorkshire Terriers have a proud past. They started out as scrappy little terriers who provided real service—and undoubtedly solace in a tough life—to the Scots immigrants who created them. They made the transition to parlor pet with ease and have experienced enormous popularity because of their adaptability and empathy for people. These scrappy, impish, intelligent, funny little dogs embody a great love for their humans that has never wavered during the more than 200 years that Yorkies and humans have been a part of each others' lives.

Celebrity Yorkies

Yorkies and celebrities seem to go together. Glamorous women from Audrey Hepburn to Eva Gabor have been endlessly photographed with their little canine companions. Tennis greats Serena and Venus Williams have Yorkies—Bob and Petey (named after tennis star Pete Sampras). Not all Yorkie fanciers are women, by any means. Brett Favre, the 230-pound Green Bay Packers quarterback, openly snuggles with his tiny Yorkie, Jazzmin. Anyone who has watched the Westminster Kennel Club dog show telecast during the years that retired baseball player and sportscaster Joe Garagiola co-hosted the event will remember him talking lovingly of his Yorkies, Sassy and Sweetie.

One of the most famous celebrity Yorkies of all time was, of course, Joan Rivers' beloved Spike, who lived to be 18. She seldom went anywhere without this dog, who was certainly photographed more than most stars.

CHARACTERISTICS
of the Yorkshire Terrier

orkies are all about character. Tough and terrier-like at one moment and the ultimate lapdog the next, Yorkies can be among the most entertaining, endearing dogs to own. It is no accident that these dogs are among the most popular breeds in both the United States and Great Britain. They are adaptable, intelligent, spunky, and they know how to capture your heart.

But like every other breed, Yorkshire Terriers don't belong in every home— and not every person is an ideal match for a Yorkie. This chapter will help you determine if the Yorkshire Terrier is the right dog for you and your family.

YORKSHIRE TERRIER APPEARANCE AND THE BREED STANDARDS

Of course, part of a Yorkie's charm is his spectacular appearance. Show dogs with dazzlingly long, silky coats are absolutely breathtaking. They draw spectators in with their bright, shiny eyes, and they sparkle with spectacular color. They are the picture of flash and élan as they skim across the floor in a brisk trot, their beautiful coats flying behind them. No doubt about it—Yorkies are a gorgeous breed.

Every breed has a standard, a blueprint that describes the height, weight, color, head, tail, and even the toes of the breed. At dog shows, every dog is judged on how well he conforms to the standard. (That is why dog show competition is often called conformation competition.) Just as no human "perfect ten" exists, no dog perfectly meets the standard for any breed. However, a Yorkie who doesn't even come close to being a show dog still can be a wonderful pet.

Why, then, should someone who just wants a pet pay attention to the standard? The standard describes, physically and temperamentally, what makes a Yorkshire Terrier different from every other breed of dog on the planet. A breeder who uses the standard as her guide will create Yorkshire Terriers who retain the hearty structure, bold temperament, and glorious coat of a well-bred Yorkie.

The breed standard describes those physical and temperamental characteristics that make the Yorkshire Terrier unique.

The following description of the Yorkshire Terrier is based on an interpretation of the American Kennel Club's breed standard. However, the American Kennel Club and Kennel Club's (England) breed standards are almost identical, which is an affirmation that Yorkies in all parts of the world will retain their unique appearance.

General Appearance

The AKC standard says that a Yorkie is a long-haired toy terrier, with a neat, compact, and well-proportioned body. The dog's high head carriage and confident manner should give the appearance of vigor and self-importance. (It's not just *your* Yorkie who is full of his own importance—the standard says that *all* Yorkies should feel that way!)

A Yorkie's crowning glory, his coat, is always parted down the middle on his face and from the base of his skull to the end of his tail. It hangs evenly and straight down each side of his body.

Head

A Yorkie's head is small, which gives him a pleasing proportion. A Yorkie has medium-sized, dark eyes "sparkling with a sharp, intelligent expression." It is that bright expression, topped off with those sharp ears, that demonstrates the heart of a terrier lurking inside your little dog. Look at a Yorkie's face, and you'll see the terrier spirit.

A Yorkie's ears are small, V-shaped, and carried erect. (They are natural ears—not cropped.)

Body

The body is well proportioned and very compact. The dog's topline is level, so his height at the shoulder is the same as his height at the rump. This description is of a hardy dog, one who will relish walks as well as win in the show ring.

Legs and Feet

The standard describes a dog with straight forelegs. He has hind legs with a moderate bend in the stifle, which move straight when viewed from behind. (When you see a great show dog with his legs moving underneath the coat with a strong, confident reach and drive, and his coat flowing behind him, you will understand the value of a little dog having the healthy body and structure the standard describes.)

Tail

The tail is docked to a medium length and carried slightly higher than the level of the back. (In the Kennel Club standard, it specifies that, while tails are customarily docked, dogs with undocked tails can be shown. An undocked tail should be as straight as possible, of a length to give a well-balanced appearance.)

A Yorkie of Another Color

The Yorkshire Terrier Club of America (YTCA) warns against buying a Yorkie with any coloring other than those described in the breed standard, including dogs who are all gold, liver (also known as red or chocolate), parti-colored, or born with a "blue" color (instead of born black).

The YTCA says, "One of the reasons for avoiding breeding 'off-colored' Yorkies is because it could be a genetic defect that may affect the dog's health. Some health problems can include, but aren't limited to, severe skin problems, allergies, total hair loss, and in some cases, long-term illness and/or death."

Even the best of breeders may, occasionally, have a puppy with improper coloring. A responsible breeder will have that puppy undergo careful health screenings. If the dog is healthy, the animal will be neutered before being placed in a home as a pet. A responsible breeder never would label that incorrect coloring as rare, exotic, or desirable.

A Yorkie puppy is born black and tan, but he will gradually change into his adult coloring.

Coat

The quality, texture, and quantity of coat are of prime importance. A Yorkie has hair that is much like human hair, and it should be glossy, fine, and silky in texture. The coat on the body is perfectly straight (not wavy). It may be trimmed to floor length to give the dog ease of movement and a neater appearance, if desired. The fall (topknot) on the head is long, tied with one bow in the center of the head or parted in the middle and tied with two bows. (Yorkies traditionally wear red bows.) The hair on the muzzle is very long. The hair should be trimmed short on the tips of ears, and it may be trimmed on the feet to give them a neat appearance.

Colors

The most distinctive characteristic of an adult Yorkshire Terrier is his long, blue and tan, silky coat. A puppy is born black and tan and gradually will change into his adult coloring. A puppy may show an intermingling of black hair in the tan until he matures.

Coat Care

The gorgeous Yorkie coat takes an enormous amount of grooming. Although show dogs sport long, luxurious coats, most people with pet Yorkies trim their dogs for much easier upkeep.

An adult Yorkie should have clear, rich coloring. The hair on the dog's head is tan, and he has tan "stockings" on his legs. The hair on his body and tail is blue. The blue is a dark steel blue, not a silver blue, and not mingled with fawn, bronze, or black hairs. The hair on the tail is a darker blue, especially at the end of the tail. All tan hair is darker at the roots than in the middle, shading to still lighter tan at the tips. There should be no sooty or black hair intermingled with any of the tan.

Size

Yorkies can come in a surprising assortment of sizes. The Yorkie standard says that the breed must weigh less than 7 pounds (3.2 kg) to compete in the conformation ring, and show dogs typically weigh between 4 and 7 pounds (1.8 and 3.2 kg). If you hope to show your Yorkie, it is important to find a dog who stays within the breed standard.

Yorkies are well suited to providing their humans with love and companionship.

Yorkie Habitats

Because Yorkies can meet their exercise needs in a small space, they make excellent apartment or condo dogs, although they happily can adjust to rule larger spaces as well.

However, as with all toy breeds, many wonderful Yorkies get a tad too big for the show ring. Even some of the most successful show breeders sometimes end up with some slightly larger Yorkies, even though their mothers or fathers are dainty little champions.

Many great Yorkies end up weighing in at 8 (3.6 kg), 10 (4.5 kg), 12 (5.4 kg), or—occasionally—even a strapping 15 pounds (6.8 kg). For some homes, these larger dogs are a better choice. The bigger dogs are less breakable, and they have less to fear from a child's overly enthusiastic hug or a somewhat larger dog's playful wrestling. If your lifestyle isn't quite right for a tiny dog, take a look at an oversized Yorkie—he might be a perfect fit.

Don't necessarily look for the tiniest Yorkie you can find. Chapter 8 discusses Yorkie health, and one of the breed's major problems is liver shunts. The most common early indication of a liver shunt is low energy and failure to grow. Dogs of any breed who weigh less than 2 pounds (0.9 kg) very rarely live long or healthy lives. For some reason, miniaturization frequently leads to health problems when dogs get that tiny. (At the other end of the spectrum, dogs who weigh more than about 150 pounds [68 kg] also experience more health problems than their slightly smaller counterparts.) Don't fall for labels like "teacups," "tinies," or "minis"—those are just advertising gimmicks designed to sell puppies to unsuspecting buyers. No classifications by size exist for this breed.

Whether a healthy 4-pound (1.8 kg) dog or a 12-pound (5.4 kg) bruiser is right for your home, you can count on that fun Yorkie character and charm to make your life more interesting.

IS THE YORKSHIRE TERRIER RIGHT FOR YOU?

Go back 100 years, and your Yorkshire Terrier's ancestors were gamely killing rats. Those genes are still there, and inside your dog a game little terrier exists. You'll observe it when he sees a squirrel and wants nothing more than to fly up the fence after it. You'll feel it in the ferocity with which he plays with his favorite squeaky toys. You'll see it in the way he struts proudly on a walk.

Terriers work independently, unlike some other kinds of dogs. Border Collies have the instinct to move sheep for humans, and Golden Retrievers willingly bring their humans birds. Not terriers! They fearlessly go after ferocious game that might be bigger than they are.

Enjoy your terrier's spirit and admire it—but be prepared for it. Yorkies vary widely in just how terrier-like they are. If you have a high prey-drive Yorkie, you must be sure he's on a leash when out for a walk, because if he sees a cat or a squirrel, he'll forget you exist until he's done with the chase.

Yorkies have a zest for life that is matched by few other breeds. They are great show dogs who stack up more than their share of wins because of that élan. They make wonderful, amusing pets because of their antics and joyful, alert natures. If you're up for the challenge of a dog who looks at a rat twice his size and says, "Wow! Wouldn't it be fun to tell him who's boss?" you'll love living with a Yorkie.

Trainability

Yorkies are often labeled "stubborn"—a word that isn't really fair. A terrier must be independent and tenacious to do his work. If you train your Yorkie like a terrier, using treats, toys, and fun to teach him lessons, you'll have a great relationship with your dog. If you expect immediate obedience just because you say a command, you will be locked in an eternal battle of wills with your Yorkie.

This doesn't mean they are hard to train, though. In fact, Yorkies are very trainable, but it's important to use today's modern methods that make training a fun game. If you try to use coercion, you'll find yourself at constant odds with your dog. No mere human being has ever truly won a battle of wills with a 5-pound (2.3 kg) Yorkie! (See Chapter 6 for obedience training that is designed to work positively with your little guy's independent spirit.)

Companionability

Aside from their terrier instincts, Yorkies have a second side to their nature—200 years of being a companion dog. These loyal little dogs are among the most empathetic of dog breeds. In fact, Yorkies have an uncanny knack for taking on the personalities of their families. Gentle people seem to have gentle Yorkies, and action-oriented owners have busy little dogs.

Your Yorkie is likely to sense your moods. He'll snuggle if you don't feel well, and he'll be playful when you recover. A decidedly sweet, incredibly close relationship can be cultivated with your Yorkie.

Some Yorkshire Terriers are more tilted toward the terrier side, while others tend more to the soft side. One of the joys of finding the right Yorkie for you is to find the one who reflects not only what you are looking for, but the kind of personality you have.

Watch Dog Tendencies

Terriers tend to bark. Toy breeds tend to bark. Yorkies are toy-sized terriers, so they tend to bark a lot! The good news is that they don't usually bark very loudly, as their little lungs make pint-sized barks. Fortunately, with training, you can reduce your Yorkie's ongoing commentary. Still, if you crave quiet, this "verbally gifted" breed may not be the best dog for you.

Remember, though, that your Yorkie doesn't bark just to amuse himself. He'll tell you what's going on in your neighborhood. Listen, and you'll learn to hear the difference in his bark when a friend is arriving versus a stranger, or when a cat is in the yard versus a dog. Sometimes it's nice to have your own alarm system in the house!

Exercise Levels

A big difference exists between the exercise needs of a 4-pound (1.8 kg), fine-boned, snuggly Yorkie and a 7-pound (3.2 kg) (or larger) high-energy dog. Still, even the largest Yorkie can get most of his exercise needs met by chasing toys across a living room floor, racing around a small yard, or going for a brisk walk.

Yorkie energy is hilarious to watch. Your dog, even through adulthood, will chase, run, zoom, and hunt—and then is likely to collapse in a happy heap and take a nap. Unlike some of the terrier breeds who need nonstop exercise, Yorkies like to rest after the action is done.

And the Record Goes to...

The Yorkshire Terrier is one of the smallest dog breeds, even in the Toy Group. Yorkies and Chihuahuas are constantly going nose-to-tiny-nose to capture the record for the World's Smallest Dog.

The Guinness World Record for the Smallest Living Dog (measured by height) is held as of this writing by a Yorkie named Whitney who measured 3 inches (7.6 cm) at the shoulder on November 26, 2002. She lives in Shoeburyness, Essex, England. The dog who held the record before Whitney was another Yorkie named Big Boss, who lived in Thailand. He was 4.7 inches (11.9 cm) tall.

A Yorkie named Tiny Pinocchio, whose owner lives in Florida, was the smallest dog (measured by length) until July 2004, when the title went to a Chihuahua named Danka Kordak, who lives in Revuca, Slovakia. Tiny Pinocchio measured 8 inches (20.3 cm) long; Danka Kordak is 7.4 inches (18.8 cm) long.

Although it is amusing to see who breaks the world record, tiny dogs are usually less healthy than those who weigh about 3 pounds (1.4 kg) or more. Look for a moderately sized Yorkie for a pet. He still will be a very small dog!

Yorkies at a Glance

- **Size?** Less than 7 pounds (3.2 kg), according to the breed standard. Sometimes oversized Yorkies make a better choice for families with children or other pets.
- **Good apartment dogs?** Yes!
- **Good for traveling?** Yes!
- **Grooming needs?** High to very high.
- **Good with children?** Generally not good with small children.
- **Good with other dogs?** Not a good mix with large dogs, but can be good friends with other small dogs.
- **Good with cats?** Depends on the temperament of the Yorkie and the cat.
- **Exercise needs?** Minimal to modest.

Remember that even the smallest Yorkie needs exercise—just as every living creature does. It's easy to just pick up your teeny guy and carry him. However, make sure that he gets exercise every day that allows him to run and play and pant, just like the big guys. You want his heart and lungs to be healthy well into his teens!

Grooming Requirements

You may have fallen in love with that flowing, shimmering coat you see at dog shows, but it takes hours of dedicated work every week to keep that kind of glorious coat. Don't even dream about it if you aren't willing to spend more time on your dog's hairdo than your own.

Most Yorkies are kept in either a puppy clip (a short version of the longer show coat) or a Schnauzer clip (with a shaved back and face—looking more like a typical terrier). Even these comparatively easy 'dos take effort, though. Yorkie hair is easily tangled, and daily brushing and combing is an absolute requirement. Even if you take your dog to a groomer, you will need to keep the dog combed daily between grooming visits.

If you use a professional groomer (which most pet owners do), it also can add up to hundreds of dollars of expense during the year. Do not consider a Yorkie for a pet if you want a simple, "wash and wear" kind of dog.

Yorkies and Children

Very young children and tiny, fine-boned dogs are a bad

Because Yorkies have tiny, delicate bones, children should be extra careful when interacting with them.

combination. Children under the age of about seven usually cannot fully distinguish between a stuffed animal and a live dog. Even a lovely, well-behaved child might hug, chase, or carry a Yorkie in a way that could injure the dog.

Young Children

Children—and adults, for that matter—should play with a Yorkie puppy while sitting on the floor. Yorkie puppies have very delicate little bones, and many young dogs have broken their legs when they decided to take a flying leap from the arms of a standing person.

It is possible that any tiny dog, including a Yorkie, will reach up and bite a child who is squeezing him. Add to a Yorkie's physical smallness that hard-wired terrier temperament, and this breed usually is not a good fit for a family with young kids. If you have small children, look for a larger, sturdier breed. (Small dogs who generally do well with gentle, well-behaved children include Pugs, Cavalier King Charles Spaniels, Shih Tzu, and Bichon Frises.) Your child will have a better time playing with a sturdier dog, and the sturdier breeds will enjoy your child in return.

Most responsible Yorkie breeders are reluctant to sell a dog to a household with small children. Some will make an exception after meeting the children, especially if a puppy or adult dog in their litter seems to especially like kids. Finding the right Yorkie for a family with young children takes a lot of effort, though.

Older Children

Older children and Yorkies can be a winning combination. They are fun dogs to train in agility and obedience, and a special camaraderie can develop between older, responsible children and a lap-sized dog. Remember, though, that kids are kids, and even the best child might not attend to details as an adult would.

Do not ever let a dog suffer because a child loses interest in caring for the animal! If you allow your child to have a pet, you must be willing to step in and care for the Yorkie if your child can't or won't do the job. Letting an animal suffer to teach the child a "lesson" only teaches your child that a pet's feelings and physical comfort don't really matter. That's not what you want a child to learn.

Yorkies and Other Dogs

Yorkies are notorious for assaulting dogs who are ten times—or more—their size. While this may seem cute and amusing, it isn't. It is the fastest way for your dog to lose his life. Yorkshire Terriers who are properly socialized with other dogs from the time they are youngsters are far less likely to get into this kind of trouble.

The more experienced your puppy is in social interaction with other dogs, the less likely he is to get into trouble. Start out by

Two Sides of One Breed

Since the late 1800s, Yorkies have been popular, pampered pets. That 100 years of living as a beloved house pet has had an impact on the breed today, just as 100 years of being a tough terrier is still deep in the genes of your little Yorkie. Perhaps no other breed is such a mixture of tough determination and absolute sweetness, independence and dependence, activity and domesticity.

Some Yorkies definitely tend to be more like their terrier roots—fiercely independent and prey-driven, always hoping for their big break when they'll be allowed to hunt a squirrel in the backyard or the mice for sale at a local pet supply shop.

Other Yorkies seem to be more comfortable as ladies' lap dogs, preferring their one special human to any other. You must understand these two aspects of Yorkie history as you choose your dog, and you must decide which personality you want to predominate in your pup.

Yorkies get along well with most birds, but be sure to supervise them when they interact with larger birds, like parrots.

leaving him with his breeder until he is 12 weeks old so that he has learned to play appropriately with littermates under his mother's watchful eye. Also, seek out other small dogs for your Yorkie to play with. Check with other Yorkie owners in your community, and invite a couple over for a play date. Other small, playful breeds like Toy Poodles, Maltese, Papillons, and Pomeranians can make good friends for play dates with your little guy.

Playing With Big Dogs

Under no circumstances should you allow your Yorkie to play with a dog who is substantially bigger than he is. He will learn an overly aggressive style of play, which can lead to very bad results with a less tolerant dog. (Also, other small dogs won't want to play with a dog with an over-the-top, aggressive play style.) Remember, too, that even a friendly, sweet dog who really is your Yorkie's buddy can break your dog's delicate bones in play. Don't take that risk. You can let them go for walks together or hang out peaceably together, but you never should allow wrestling, chase games, or nipping.

Behaving With Other Dogs

Too many small dog owners think it's funny or even adorable when their little dogs bark or charge at big dogs. It's not. The big dog is likely to respond to your Yorkie's aggression with his own aggression—and the big dog wins. It's not acceptable for a Rottweiler or a Doberman Pinscher to snarl, snap, and lunge at another dog, and it's not acceptable for your Yorkie to, either.

Living With Big Dogs

In most cases, it is not a great idea to have Yorkies living with large dogs. Yorkies like to rule the roost, and if the big dog gets irked, he can endanger your Yorkie's life. If you are considering having a Yorkie living with a maxi-sized dog, take special precautions. Make clear rules and keep them. Don't let the dogs take each other's toys, and don't ever tolerate snapping or growling from either dog. A scene that would be a minor squabble between same-size siblings can become a calamity when one dog is small and the other dog is large.

Even if your Yorkie and your big bruiser are best buddies, don't leave them loose together when they are unsupervised. All it takes is a misplaced paw or an out-of-control skid while they're playing tag, and you'll come home to tragedy.

Yorkies and Other Animals

Let's start with rodents. Yorkies were originally bred to hunt rodents, and the desire to kill mice, rats, and anything that reminds the dog of those creatures is hard-wired into your Yorkie's heart. If someone in your family loves her gerbils, hamsters, or pet mice, a Yorkie might not be a judicious addition to your household. If a family member has rodents for pets, make sure your Yorkie isn't allowed in the room where the other animals live, and that the animals are securely kept in their cages or enclosures.

Most birds and Yorkies can get along well, but be sure that the bird has a safe haven from the dog. Don't let the Yorkie have access to a bird whose wings are clipped and can't get away, because some Yorkies will think they have been given a feathered toy. Also, large birds, such as some parrots, can hurt a Yorkie, so keep both animals separate enough to be safe.

Cats and Yorkies usually end up the very best of friends. Watch larger Yorkies to make sure they don't hunt the cat, and supervise larger cats to make sure they don't hunt the Yorkie.

You may first be attracted to the Yorkshire Terrier because of his attractive, elegant appearance, but you'll stay in love with the dog who's under the hair. It is the heart of the dog that matters most, and no breed of dog has more heart than a Yorkshire Terrier!

Size Matters

Your little Yorkie may act like a big dog, but he can end up seriously hurt, or worse, if he ends up fighting—or even playing too roughly—with an actual big dog. Always supervise your Yorkie's play with larger dogs or other animals.

PREPARING
for Your Yorkshire Terrier

Y ou've made the big decision: A Yorkie is the right dog for you. It's important to remember, though, that romance doesn't end up "happily ever after" once you fall in love. It takes work, dedication, and planning. The same is true for your dog. If you take care now, you'll have a lifetime of happy, bonded, and loving times ahead. In fact, selecting the right Yorkie for you, preparing for him, and getting him off to a healthy start will make all the difference in the world.

PRELIMINARY DECISIONS

One of the advantages to owning a purebred dog is that you can be pretty sure how your dog will grow up to look and act. The guidelines created by the standard give Yorkies their relative uniformity across the nation and even around the world. Even if you would never dream of owning a show dog, and if you never go to a dog show, purchase your dog or puppy from a source that cares about breeding to the standard.

After you have decided to purchase your purebred Yorkshire Terrier, two of the most important decisions you'll have to make are whether to purchase a male or female or a puppy or adult dog.

Male Versus Female

Don't worry about looking for a male or female—look for the right dog for you. Some fanciers say that females tend to be more aloof and that males tend to be friendlier and cuddlier. However, plenty of cuddly females exist, as well as lots of independent-minded males. Choose a dog who captures your heart, and don't worry about the "plumbing."

Purchasing a puppy can be very rewarding, but it's also a lot of work.

Puppy Versus Adult

Most people buy puppies—and there is a lot of joy to that. Purchasing a puppy gives you the opportunity to make sure that your little guy gets a great start in life. You'll have the chance to make sure he gets wonderful socialization and learns to be confident and happy with people and other animals.

Still, puppies can be overrated. They require round-the-clock attention, and you have to deal with housetraining, chewing, and teething. In fact, for working people, the demands of a puppy can be impossible.

Because Yorkies usually live well into their teens, you might want to consider getting an adult. The big fear most people have about getting an adult is that the older dog won't bond to them as well as a puppy. Ask anyone who's adopted an older dog, though, and they'll tell you the opposite is true. Older dogs seem to know when they've been picked by their special someone, and they have a depth of commitment to their people that a puppy just can't match. If they've been rescued from a sad situation, that joy and love is even bigger. One rescuer who sings the praises of bringing home older dogs says, "You can become so bonded to an older dog, you'll swear you gave birth to him."

Many show breeders have "change of career" dogs who make extraordinary pets. The dog may be a 12-month-old teenager who was kept as a show prospect but didn't quite materialize into a top winner. The dog might be a retired champion or a brood bitch who is retired and wants to be somebody's "only" dog. A breeder should provide registration papers, health records, and related information for an older dog, just as she would a puppy.

Adult Yorkies usually adjust very quickly to loving new homes, and many people find the joy of bringing home a grown-up dog to be even greater than the fun of getting a puppy.

Pet Versus Show Quality

Some of the best pet puppies are dogs who don't quite make the grade as show dogs. A pet-quality dog might not have just the right coloring in his coat, or his tail set may be a little too high, or his ears may be a little too big. He might be just a bit too large or too small to be competitive in the show ring. These tiny cosmetic differences are almost invisible to someone who doesn't show dogs, even after the breeder points out the differences. Despite the fact that he never will be able to compete in the show ring, you still will have a gorgeous little pet who will look like a show dog to you.

If you are buying a "pet-quality" puppy or adult from a show breeder, do ask why the puppy isn't show quality. Some reasons that a dog won't do well in the show ring can affect his quality as a pet. If the dog is too shy to enjoy showing, he might not be happy in a boisterous household. If his toes face all four directions, he's not a good prospect for agility competition, a demanding sport that demands excellent structure. Most show breeders want what's best for their dogs, and they will work very hard to find just the right home for their well-bred "pet-quality" dogs.

You also might get the chance to purchase a show dog. Be aware, though, that a show dog requires an extraordinary amount of coat care! If you are paying for a show-quality dog, be sure that you are really getting what you're paying for. Only buy a "show dog" from someone who actively and successfully shows in the

Neutering

Unless you are seriously committed to breeding good-quality dogs, which is a world of its own, you must neuter your new pet. Reputable breeders will require neutering, and an increasing number are neutering their puppies before they are sold.

ring. Otherwise, you may be purchasing a pet-quality dog at a show-quality price.

WHERE TO PURCHASE YOUR YORKSHIRE TERRIER

It matters where you buy your Yorkie! Yorkies are among the most popular of dog breeds. Unfortunately, they are also a favorite among puppy-mill breeders—people who breed only for profit and who don't care about the happiness of the dogs or the future of the breed. It is very important, then, to do your research and determine the best source for your family's new Yorkshire Terrier.

Breeders

The first few weeks in your dog's life are among the most important. What happens during that time will hugely affect your dog's long-term health, his ability to accept new situations and new people, his attitude toward other dogs, and even his ability to learn and think. The only person who can make sure that your puppy gets a good start to life is his breeder.

Responsible breeders take good care of their dogs, and want to make sure you will provide the best possible care for the dog you purchase from them.

Scientists have identified critical periods in puppy development. They've proved that puppies with confident, nurturing mothers, varied appropriate experiences with new places, and certain kinds of interactions with humans grow up to be healthier, happier, and even smarter than puppies who don't have these experiences. Good breeders know and understand this. Their puppies are touched and held from the day they are born, and they are socialized with gentle children and adults. They also have the chance to play with their littermates and learn from their mom, because they don't leave their home until they're at least 12 weeks old.

If you decide to go with a breeder, it's in your best interest—and the best interest of your dog, as well as the breed—to buy from the very best, most responsible breeder that you can find. If you have to wait for a puppy from that great breeder, do it. It's a lot better than an impulse buy from someone who will have given your dog a bad start in life.

Signs of Responsible and Irresponsible Breeders

Some indications that the breeder is a caring, responsible person who's giving her Yorkies a great start in life include:

- The puppies are well cared for. The puppies and the mother are clean, and so are any other dogs who live in the home. They live inside the breeder's house and have access to outside play areas that are clean and healthy. Too many people who breed Yorkies leave their dogs in small cages 24 hours a day. While using crates at bedtime and keeping females in heat separate from

Puppy Buyer Checklist

The following is a good checklist that will help you determine what you need from the breeder when purchasing your Yorkie.

- The puppy's parents should be AKC registered, and the breeder should supply a registration slip, limited registration, or agreement to register the puppy after the neutering is complete.
- The breeder has provided a copy of the puppy's pedigree.
- If a contract is provided, you have read it and understand it.
- The puppy has started his vaccinations, and you have been given a copy of the schedule to give to your veterinarian.
- You have discussed the puppy's diet, and you have food ready for the puppy (either provided by the breeder or purchased before picking up the puppy).
- You have the breeder's phone number in case you have any questions or problems.

A breeder's puppies should appear healthy and well cared for.

males are good, ethical practices, keeping animals confined in small cages all day is cruel.

- You don't feel bad at the thought of this breeder breeding more dogs. It's easy to feel sorry for a puppy and decide to "rescue" him from a sad situation. Unfortunately, all you've accomplished is to line the pockets of an unethical breeder. If she makes money on a litter, she will just breed another. Don't give your money to anyone whose dogs live in unhappy, unclean, unpleasant conditions. Instead, buy your puppy from someone who raises her dogs with love and care. Anything else merely supports a cycle of abuse and neglect for these wonderful little dogs.

- The breeder is willing to take a dog back if you can't keep him. They care about their puppies throughout the life of the dog.

- A good breeder will be extremely knowledgeable about the breed and the heritage of her dogs. She probably shows her dogs. She can show you generations of pedigrees and can explain exactly why she bred one dog to another. She's also usually a member of the national breed club and subscribes to its code of ethics.

The following warning signs are a tip-off that you're not working with an ethical breeder. Think twice, and think again, before buying a dog if:

- The breeder advertises "teacup" Yorkies. Yorkies are less than 7 pounds (3.18 kg), according to the breed standard—that is already a very small dog. Trying to make a tiny breed even tinier is a cause for health concern, most especially potentially fatal liver shunts. Plus, advertising "teacups" is a marketing gimmick designed to snare naïve, unknowledgeable buyers. Don't be that buyer!

- The parents aren't AKC registered, and the puppies don't have a litter registration. The AKC has minimal health and record-keeping standards for high-volume breeders. If the puppies you are looking at aren't registered, there's a good chance this breeder fails to meet those standards.

  Be especially leery of dogs who are registered with any registry other than the AKC. The AKC has minimum standards for large breeders. Because these standards take some effort to meet, some of the worst breeders created their own "kennel clubs" so that they could tell unsuspecting, naïve buyers that the dogs were "registered." The bottom line should be no AKC registration, no sale.

- The breeder suggests meeting you someplace other than her home. A good breeder will be proud to show you the sparkling, clean, happy place her puppies live. She wouldn't dream of meeting someone at a park or freeway rest stop to sell a puppy.

- The breeder sells puppies before they are 12 weeks old. Yorkie puppies are tiny. For health and safety reasons, good breeders keep their puppies until they are 12 weeks old with very, very rare exceptions. Be suspicious of anyone selling a Yorkie puppy who is less than 12 weeks old. Do not, under any circumstances, bring home a puppy less than 10 weeks old. You are asking for

Yorkie Health Issues

The best breeders will screen potential breeding stock for Progressive Retinal Atrophy (PRA) before each breeding (males will be screened annually if they breed more than once a year), and these breeders will register the results with the Canine Eye Registry Foundation (CERF). Good breeder also will have their dogs' kneecaps (patellas) checked, and they will register those results with the Orthopedic Foundation for Animals (OFA).

Talk with the breeder about the health problems that occur in the breed, and ask what she does to breed dogs who are as healthy as possible. No breeder can guarantee that every dog will be perfect, but she will work hard toward that goal.

A responsible breeder will have at least the mother of the puppies on the premises and will encourage you to meet her.

problems.

- The breeder is reluctant to have you meet her other dogs. A good breeder is thrilled with her contribution to the world of dogs. If she is hesitant for you to meet her other dogs, this is a signal that something is wrong.
- The breeder has too many dogs or dogs of several breeds. Serious breeders usually limit their breeding to one or two breeds and become true experts in their own breeds. A good hobby breeder may have more dogs than most people, but she will never have 50.
- The breeder doesn't ask questions about you and your lifestyle. Do you really want to buy a dog from someone who doesn't care about where her puppy will live?
- It doesn't feel right. If you get a bad feeling about the place and the puppies, you don't owe an explanation to anyone. Just say that you're still looking, and walk away. Trust your instincts about whether this breeder has the best interests of the puppies

at heart.

With the demand right now for toy dogs, it's easy to get frustrated. Some breeders have long waiting lists for their Yorkies. It's better to wait a year and get a puppy who has been loved, socialized, and given a great start in life. Promise yourself—and your new puppy—that you will wait for a kind and loving breeder when you buy your Yorkie. Don't give your money to anyone who doesn't have the best interests of the dog at heart.

Finding a Great Breeder

With just a little effort and some minor homework, you can find the kind of breeder who gives her puppies a great start. One place to look is your local breed club's website, many of which list breeders who are club members who have agreed to a code of ethics. Of course, you always should check out the breeder personally, but breeder lists can be an excellent starting point.

Another excellent place to look for a breeder is a local dog show. Talk with the people who are showing their dogs (when they're not busy), and get a sense of the dogs and the people who impress you. Make an appointment to go visit them, or get a card so that you can correspond after the show. Every show has a catalog for sale that includes the name and mailing address for every exhibitor; this is a great way to contact prospective breeders. You also can talk to people at the show's information desk to see if any local club members are Yorkie breeders. People active in their local club are often wonderful breeders.

While you are at the show, you might want to check to see if any Yorkshire Terriers are entered in the obedience or agility competitions that often accompany all-breed shows. These competitors usually select their dogs based on their temperaments and physical soundness, and they may be able to tell you where they bought their dogs.

The American Kennel Club website now has classified ads that feature breeders with puppies to sell. The AKC asks the breeders to create a profile of themselves. You, as a consumer, can decide if this breeder has the kind of ethics that make you want to purchase a dog. The breeder profile will tell you if the breeder:

• Provides AKC registration applications to the puppy buyer.
• Is a member of the Yorkshire Terrier Club of America and/or a local affiliate of the YTCA.

Choose Wisely

Don't buy a Yorkie (or any other dog) from someone who will sell her animals to the first person with a credit card. This person probably doesn't have the best interests of the dog in mind.

- Is a member of a local dog club.
- Performed health screenings on the litter's parents.
- Provides a written bill of sale detailing the responsibilities of both the buyer and the seller.
- Takes back a puppy under all conditions if the buyer can no longer keep the dog.
- Provides the puppy buyer with information about exercise, training, feeding, immunizations, proper veterinary care, and responsible dog ownership.
- Provides a health guarantee for the puppy.
- Permanently identifies all his or her breeding stock by microchip or tattoo.
- Competes in AKC events such as conformation, obedience, or agility.
- Has been breeding for less than 5 years, 5 to 10 years, 11 to 20 years, or more than 20 years.

Several Internet chat lists exist for Yorkie fanciers, and once in a while, they can help you find a good breeder. You can have virtual conversations with Yorkie lovers around the world. This can be a very good way to get acquainted with the breed, and often breeders participate in the discussions. Some of the top names among Yorkie breeders occasionally share their perspectives online with newcomers to the breed. However, Yorkies are just like any other subject on the Internet, so be skeptical of what people tell you. You may never know whether the person who is giving you her opinion is a world-renowned Yorkie expert or is widely regarded by other breeders as a crackpot. Check out any breeder you meet on the Internet with the same healthy skepticism that you would any other Internet meeting.

Occasionally, the newspaper may be a good place to find a breeder. Most good breeders don't advertise in a local paper, but sometimes they do. Evaluate people who advertise in the

Rescue Yorkies Like to Play, Too

Do you want to compete in the sports of agility, obedience, rally, or tracking with your rescue Yorkie? It used to be that only registered dogs could enter. Now, you can get an Indefinite Listing Privilege for your neutered rescue Yorkie. Just fill out a form and send verification from a veterinarian that the dog has been neutered, along with the required fee and two photos that show that he's a purebred dog. For more information, go to the American Kennel Club's website at www.akc.org.

Rescued Yorkies can make great family pets.

newspaper with the same caution that you would evaluate people who advertise cars in the newspaper. They might be great breeders, but chances are they might not be.

Visiting Breeders

Always visit your potential breeder. Internet photos or phone conversations aren't the same as taking a good look at the dog, breeder, and kennel in person and deciding if you like what you see.

Once you have the names of a couple of breeders, make an appointment to go visit them without the mission of looking for a specific puppy. See if you like the way the breeder treats her dogs. Also, get to know the adult dogs' personalities. (Remember, the personality of the puppy will be formed by the combination of his

Before you buy, think. Decide if a Yorkshire Terrier is the right dog for you. Think about the person who is selling the dog and whether she is a person who has the best interests of this wonderful little breed at heart. Pick the particular dog who fits your expectations and your lifestyle. Care enough about your dog to groom that hard-to-care-for coat, train him, and give him first-rate medical care.

genes and his early upbringing—you see both when you look at the breeder and her dogs.)

The home of even the best breeder can seem a little overwhelming. Think of it as the difference between a small family and someone with eight kids. Life is just more chaotic in larger numbers. A breeder's dogs are likely to sleep in crates at night (even small dogs like Yorkies can fill up their humans' beds pretty quickly!), and breeders have to keep intact dogs reasonably separate from each other—they don't want any unplanned pregnancies. Still, the difference between a healthy, happy multi-dog household and a place where people are breeding dogs for profit will be abundantly clear.

It doesn't matter whether you agree with the breeder's personal politics, admire her décor, or want to be her best friend (although you might find your best friend—you never know). What does matter is that you respect the way she treats her dogs and that you can communicate well, so that if you do get a puppy, you can utilize her wisdom.

Be clear about what you want in a Yorkie. This is not a uniform breed, and these dogs vary widely in personality (from cuddly to pretty darn feisty), size, and sociability. Think about the role you want your dog to play in your life before you go looking at puppies.

Also, talk with the breeder about your lifestyle and what you want in a companion. Do you have children? Do you live in a condo or in the country? Do you travel a lot? Do you work outside the home?

Expect the breeder to ask prying, probing, personal questions. She may even insist on coming to your home for a visit. If a breeder loves her dogs, she won't allow them to go to inappropriate homes. You should welcome these questions. A great breeder knows her dogs' souls, and she will help you find the right dog for your circumstances. She can't help you if you don't tell her what you want in a pet, and she certainly can't tell you if you aren't honest.

Rescue Me!

Sadly, a lot of people buy Yorkies on a whim, only to realize that this breed isn't the right one for them. Some of these owners drop their dogs off at a shelter without a second thought and never look back. Other Yorkies had loving families, but illness or other unexpected problems made it impossible for these families to care for their beloved pets. Sometimes puppy mills dump their dogs after they aren't useful for breeding any more.

The bottom line is that although a few puppies end up in rescue, a wide variety of dogs, from young adults to oldsters, desperately need great homes. Some may have special needs, such as medical problems or behavioral issues. Others are shy and need an understanding owner who will devote the time and love to help them through their problems. Still others are friendly, well-adjusted, and ready to start life anew.

Responsible rescue groups care about the future of the dogs in their care. They've seen how hard it is for these dogs to be handed from home to home, and they want the adoptive home to be a permanent one.

Responsible rescue groups *always* will require you to neuter your dog. In fact, most are now neutering their Yorkies before they go to their new homes. They also will tell you in exhausting detail

Some rescue Yorkies may have special needs or behavioral issues, but these Yorkies can be happy, loving additions to homes in which their needs are met.

Making the Right Choice

Before you pick your puppy, you may want to visit him with his mother and littermates more than once and observe him in different situations. Spend time with him alone to see how comfortable he is with you, but also watch him and his littermates at play. Doing so will help you get a better idea of the personality of the puppy you will be welcoming into your home.

just what problems the rescue Yorkie may have. They will check out your home extensively and may ask for references from your veterinarian. They do all this because they want these dogs with a sad past to have the best possible future. You may decide to be part of the indescribable joy of being that future for a Yorkie in need!

Finding a Rescue Yorkie

No one cares more about the future of the breed than the responsible breeders who are members of many local Yorkie breed clubs. These members are devoted to helping any Yorkie find a safe and loving home. You can find various contacts for organizations such as the Yorkshire Terrier Club of America online at www.ytca.org.

One fabulous website, www.petfinder.com, is the answer to many dreams. Rescue groups and shelters post animals available for adoption, and people looking for a pet can find the perfect match. Simply go to www.petfinder.com, select Yorkshire Terrier, and give your zip code. Yorkies looking for homes from rescue groups around the United States will come up on your screen. These listings are complete with photos, histories, and special needs (if any). The listings closest to your home even pop up first. This is a great way to find a pet!

Yorkies are among the most popular breeds in the country, and local shelters often find themselves with a Yorkie looking for a home. These adorable little guys are usually adopted quickly, so the best idea is to tell your local shelter that you'd like to be notified if a Yorkie arrives. Many shelters keep "wish lists" for people looking for specific breeds.

Before You Adopt

Every Yorkie who lands in a rescue group has a story of his own. Some were well-loved and well-cared-for dogs whose owners died. Others were living lives of misery until they were dumped somewhere. Still others were surrendered because of health concerns.

Find out what you can about the dog's story before you adopt. If you have children, you want to make sure the dog doesn't have problems with aggression, because kids and a dog who bites aren't a happy combination. If the dog has health concerns, be sure you're able and willing to deal with those problems before you adopt the dog.

PICKING THE RIGHT PUPPY FOR YOU

The Yorkie you choose should have bright, clear eyes and a healthy coat.

The day has finally come! You've done your homework and found a great source for your Yorkie, and now you're ready to find the dog to share your life. This is made a little more challenging because Yorkies, like other toy dogs, have very small litters—usually only two or three puppies. You must select the best Yorkie for you with both your heart and your head.

Keep your dream dog firmly in mind, and he will find you. It may happen on the first litter you meet, and it may happen on the tenth. You'll know it when it happens. Your puppy will choose you just as much as you choose your puppy. You'll feel the sense of kinship and rapport, and you'll be bonded from that very first meeting.

Buying a Show Dog

You might be toying with the possibility of getting a show dog. After all, dog shows are now a hit on television, and you can see that it's an exciting, rewarding, sometimes thrilling hobby. It also can be expensive.

If you think you might want a show dog, first things first. Become a student of the breed. Don't just leap into purchasing a show dog because someone says the dog is show-quality. Before considering purchasing a show dog, you should do the following:

- *Study and begin to understand the breed standard.* This blueprint of the breed describes the ideal Yorkshire Terrier from his nose to his toes, his ears to his tail. Know what's in it. However, the breed standard has been compared to the Constitution of the United States—it's a relatively small document that is interpreted by judges. Knowing the standard backward and forward is just the beginning.

- *Think about your dog's lifestyle.* Show dogs take a breathtaking amount of coat care to keep those long, flowing, shimmering tresses rewarded in the show ring. This takes time, expertise, and supervision so that your dog doesn't do things to tear his coat. Your dog will live in wrappers in his off time. (See Chapter 5 for a hint of what grooming a Yorkie is like.)

- *Go to dog shows.* Watch the dogs and the judging. Try to understand what makes one dog win more often than others. Pay close attention to the "specials," the champions who are shown with the hopes of group placements and Best in Show wins. Remember, a Yorkie is judged on much more than that wondrous show coat. He's judged on movement, expression, and the shape of his head—the total dog. Sometimes, the important judging criteria are camouflaged by the hair, and it's only by really getting to know the breed and the individual dog that you'll understand what makes one a famous champion and the other go home without the ribbons.

- *Get to know the exhibitors in your area.* Talk with them about what it's like to show dogs. As you become acquainted with local Yorkie show people, find someone you like and trust, and discuss the possibility of finding a show prospect to get you started.

Show breeders aren't going to sell their very best show prospects to the first stranger who comes along, and they aren't likely to sell a potential champion with no strings attached. Expect an agreement (insist that it's in writing) that details what the breeder expects of you and what you can expect from the breeder. It probably will require you to show your dog at a specific minimum number of shows. It may require you to hire a professional handler if you aren't successful at showing the dog yourself.

The contract is likely to include requirements about breeding the dog, and the breeder may have the rights to one or more future puppies from your dog. The breeder may want to maintain co-ownership of the dog. Look at the agreement closely, and think long and hard before you sign it.

Showing a dog is the thrill of a lifetime for many Yorkie lovers, but it's something to go into with your eyes wide open, and only with people you respect and trust.

Appearance

Start out with an overall impression of the puppy's physical structure and health. Are his eyes bright? Is his coat shiny? Is his energy level good? A Yorkie with chronic health problems isn't the best choice for a pet for most families. Be especially concerned if the puppy is especially tiny and seems to lack energy. Recent studies have concluded that 3 percent of Yorkies have liver shunts. (See Chapter 8 for a discussion of this serious health problem.) Far more Yorkies have this condition than any other breed of dog. The most obvious sign of this often fatal condition is a lack of growth and energy in a puppy.

Adult Yorkies also should appear healthy. Look for a shiny coat, lively eyes, and a friendly demeanor. Watch for the dog's gait when he runs—any skipping or limping motion can be a sign of a luxating patella, which may involve expensive surgery to repair.

If the adult is a rescue dog and he doesn't look healthy, ask what health issues have been identified. It's wonderful to rescue an adult dog who needs you, but it's important to do so with an awareness of the issues you may have to face.

Temperament

Watch the puppies play and rest. A puppy may seem calm and easygoing when you first meet him, but that may just mean he's ready for a nap. It's a good idea to visit the puppies more than once in order to get a feeling for their overall personalities.

Take each puppy away from his mom and littermates into a different room where he doesn't usually spend a lot of time. See how he bonds with you. Talk with him. Offer some toys to him, and see how he responds. Beware of the puppy who doesn't want to make eye contact with you or avoids you. This puppy might be shy, sick, or in pain. In any event, the dog isn't bonding with you.

Keep in mind the adult dog you dreamed about when you decided you wanted a Yorkie. Do you want the cuddly adult dog who desires nothing more than to snuggle with you for hours on end? If so, pick the puppy who settles into your arms like it's the place he was born to be. Do you like the feisty little adult terrier wrapped in Yorkie fur? Then select the puppy who shakes his little toys and chews on your socks.

With an adult Yorkie, what you see is what you get. Do you like a confident little guy? Then look for one who walks up to you and demands your attention. A shy dog might warm up eventually, but this could take a long time.

The bottom line is to take the time to get to know the dog. Play with him, hold him, and see if he seems to speak to you. If you don't feel a profound connection, wait for the next dog. You will find the perfect Yorkie for you, so take your time until you find him.

Socialization

Ask the breeder about the puppies' socialization. Some breeders

Registering Your Yorkshire Terrier in England

Registering your dog with the Kennel Club is almost identical to registering a dog with the American Kennel Club. Both parents must be registered, and the breeder must register the litter. The breeder will give you a registration certificate that you will fill out and the Kennel Club will process.

The Kennel Club, like the AKC, now includes some perks with registration, including an initial period of free health insurance for your puppy. For more information, check out the Kennel Club website at www.the-kennel-club.org.uk.

Make sure your Yorkie has a comfy place to sleep.

say their puppies are well socialized (and might even believe it), even though their puppies have merely lived in an exercise pen in the kitchen. By the time they are ready to go to their new homes (at 12 weeks or older for a small dog like a Yorkie), the puppies should have been handled by people of all ages, including children. They should have been exposed to a variety of floor surfaces, such as carpet and linoleum. Weather permitting, they should have had the chance to play outside in a safe area. They also should have ridden in a car at least once.

IMPORTANT DOCUMENTS

If you've gone to a responsible source and found your soul mate wrapped in fur, you've done a great job. However, a few important documents still must be obtained and discussed with the seller. These include health records, registration papers, pedigree, contract, and feeding instructions.

Health Records

While the puppy is nursing, his mother's milk provides him

Multiple-Yorkie Households

Many Yorkie owners come to a realization: They don't want just one. Two Yorkies really can be more fun than one, and they usually enjoy having a best friend. They will entertain each other, and most will play endless games of tag, tug, and zoomies.

Some Yorkies are aggressive with other dogs, particularly those of the same sex. If you have one of those dogs, it's best to get a Yorkie of the opposite gender (neutered, of course!). However, more often than not, two Yorkies of the same gender can become good friends.

It's best to wait until you've had your first Yorkie for about a year before considering a second one. This will give you plenty of time to form a close bond with your first dog and to know his personality well so that you can pick a good buddy for him.

How you treat the interactions between both dogs during the first few days may determine whether they become mortal enemies or best friends. Here are some tips:

- **Introduce them on neutral territory.** One of the worst mistakes an owner can make is to bring the new puppy (or adult) right into the house. The newcomer has just waltzed into your Yorkie's territory—and remember, these are territorial little dogs. Ideally, you can do a meet and greet with your dog and the prospective new one someplace neutral, like an area of the breeder's house the puppy doesn't usually go to, or a get-acquainted room at the shelter.

  If that isn't practical, at least take both dogs on a walk before you bring the new dog inside the house, and let them decide they like each other on neutral turf. If they are buddies, or at least tolerate each other in a neutral place, then the two dogs are likely to have a good relationship when they come home together.

- **Pay special attention to your first dog.** A good rule of thumb is to give the existing dog 75 percent of the attention for the first two weeks. The last thing you want to do is to have the older dog feel left out and jealous of the new dog. If you do this, you'll see your older dog visibly relax after several days, and you can begin giving both dogs equal attention.

  Your new puppy won't be upset by getting less attention at first than the older one; after all, he's used to sharing attention with his littermates and mom. He'll just be happy to have a great home with a loving human and an older dog buddy.

  Throughout the lifetime of the two dogs, remind the older dog of his importance to you by greeting him first, feeding him first, and always setting aside special alone time together.

- **Make the dogs' time together fun.** When you're playing with the puppy, give the older dog lots of attention and treats. Play games with both of them at once, and laugh and have a good time with both dogs. If good things happen every time the older dog is with the younger dog, he's more likely to enjoy having this new buddy.

Most Yorkies become deeply devoted to their new four-footed family member within a couple of weeks. Two dogs really can be twice as much fun as one. If you have room in your heart and in your house for a second terrific little terrier, it can be a great joy.

Two Yorkies can be twice the fun as one, but it's a good idea to wait until you've had your first Yorkie for about a year before adding another to your household.

Supplies at a Glance

The following is a list of supplies you will need to have ready for your new Yorkie's arrival:

- Leash and collar/harness
- Food and water bowls
- Grooming supplies
- Crate
- Exercise pen/baby gate
- Identification
- Toys

with immunity from most diseases. After that time, vaccinations give your puppy his own immunity. Puppies are given a series of vaccinations from the age of six weeks to about four months. Be sure to get the list of vaccinations that your puppy has received and give it to your veterinarian so that she can keep your puppy fully immunized.

Registration Papers

The breeder or seller should show you that both of the puppy's parents are AKC registered and that she has a litter registration for the puppies. The litter registration provides a form for each puppy; when you send that individual registration application to the AKC, the puppy will become a registered dog.

A responsible breeder or seller may do one of four things with your puppy's registration:

1. She may give you the registration application for the puppy. If so, you then name your puppy and send the form to the AKC. Talk with your breeder to be sure she doesn't have any requirements for your puppy's registered name. For example, some breeders ask all of the dogs in the litter to have names starting with the same letter of the alphabet. Others have themes, such as flowers, classical music, or sports cars. Others like a name that reflects a famous parent or grandparent.

2. She may give you a neuter contract that allows you to get the registration application after your pet has been altered. This practice is increasingly common among good breeders. As soon as you show your breeder that your pup has been neutered, you will receive the form to send to the AKC to register your dog.

3. She may give you a limited registration. This option is also increasingly common. A limited registration allows you to compete in obedience, agility, and other performance sports and is evidence that you have a purebred dog. However, you can't compete in conformation shows, and if your dog were ever to have puppies, the puppies couldn't be registered.

4. She already may have registered the dog. Some breeders like to register all of their own puppies. This allows the breeder to give the dog his official, registered name. The breeder will sign the AKC registration papers over to you at the sale (or after neutering if that is the agreement).

All of these options are typical of a reputable breeder. Make

to neuter your puppy before you can receive your AKC papers. It should require you to return the puppy to the breeder if you decide not to keep the dog—a step that responsible breeders take to ensure their puppies don't later end up in shelters. The contract is also likely to contain health guarantees. Understand what you are agreeing to, and be sure you feel comfortable with the arrangement.

Feeding Instructions

If your puppy is younger than six months old, he's probably eating three times a day. Be sure to get a feeding schedule from your breeder, and find out what kind of food your puppy is eating. You'll want to keep the puppy eating the same food on the same schedule, at least for the first week or two.

PREPARING YOUR HOME FOR THE NEW ARRIVAL

You know a Yorkie is the perfect dog for you, and you've found the perfect Yorkie. Now it's time for a little retail therapy. Yes, shopping! What could be more fun than buying little things for your little dog? The following are some supplies you'll need to get you started.

Leash and Collar or Harness

As toy breeds are becoming more popular, it's getting easier to find a leash and collar that is the appropriate size for a Yorkie. A tiny little dog with a huge leash and collar looks pretty bedraggled, and he certainly won't enjoy a walk as much as a dog with a light collar and small leash will.

Major pet supply companies, catalogs, and online pet supply stores have a growing number of small collars. Be sure to get a dog collar and not a cat collar, because cat collars usually have a breakaway mechanism for a cat's safety. The last thing you want your Yorkie's collar to do is to release your dog!

Your little Yorkie doesn't need a choke or prong collar—a small buckle collar will be fine. The new, adjustable collars that have a plastic snap are also great for growing puppies.

Many people with Yorkies prefer harnesses to collars. They don't put any pressure on the dog's throat. A well-fitted, comfortable little harness is just as good a choice as a collar. Choose whatever seems to work best for you and your dog.

Finding slender leashes with tiny, lightweight hooks is more of

Small Packages

Pretty much every item you purchase for your Yorkie will have to be tailored to his small size. This includes everything from his leash and collar to his food dish and even toys. (Your Yorkie may like his toys giant-size, but his little mouth will have quite a bit of trouble with a typical tennis ball!)

Provide your Yorkie with safe toys that don't have parts that can be accidentally swallowed.

a challenge than finding small collars. If you can't find a nice leash in the dog section of your local pet supply store, try the cat section. Cat leashes tend to be light in weight, and they work well for small dogs. The best solution is to go to a dog show. You usually can find good-quality leashes for toy dogs for sale at shows.

Food and Water Bowls

Make sure the food and water bowls you purchase are small enough for your Yorkie to use comfortably. A Yorkie could take a swim in a water bowl that a full-sized dog enjoys. Your Yorkie should have fresh, clean water available at all times.

The bowl should be made of nonporous materials, such as ceramic or stainless steel. Plastic bowls develop scratches on the surface over time, which can be breeding grounds for bacteria.

Grooming Supplies

There is a variety of grooming supplies you'll want to have on hand for your Yorkie, including:

- Nail clippers
- Nonskid mat for sink
- Pin brush
- Conditioner
- Scissors to trim feet and tidy up coat

- Shampoo
- Towels
- Hair dryer
- Comb

For more information, see Chapter 5.

Crate

Before you mumble to yourself that you'll never put your Yorkie in "doggy prison," think again. A Yorkie doesn't see a crate as a cage or a jail; he views it as his den. It's a nice, quiet spot to hang out when things get too rambunctious for the little guy. A crate is also a home away from home when you travel with your dog. Crates, from the point of view of a Yorkie, are a wonderful invention.

Make sure you have the proper grooming supplies to keep your Yorkie's coat beautiful and healthy.

You want your Yorkie to enjoy his crate and view it as his personal room. Here are some tips for successfully crate training your Yorkie:

- Purchase a sturdy crate that's large enough for the dog to sit, stand, turn around, and lie down in. Folding crates such as those made by Nylabone have the added value and convenience of being easy to store away when not in use.
- Teach your dog to enjoy his crate. Start out by simply placing a dog treat in the crate and letting the dog eat the treat. Later, close the crate door briefly. Over the course of a couple of days, gradually work the dog up to staying in the crate for two-hour increments.
- Always reinforce the fact that the crate is a great place. Place it where the dog feels like part of the family, such as the living room. (If he sleeps in his crate, put a crate in the bedroom so that he gets to sleep with the

Puppy-proof your home so that your Yorkie does not have access to any items that could prove harmful.

rest of his "pack.") Feed your dog his meals in the crate.

- Never put your dog in his crate for punishment. The crate is a happy place, not the canine equivalent of Siberia.
- When you put the dog in his crate or let him out of the crate, be matter-of-fact. You aren't rescuing him from prison. He's just leaving his room and coming into the rest of the house.

Exercise Pens and Baby Gates

At times, you will need to contain your Yorkie, but you want to give him a little more freedom and space than a crate allows. For example, if you're gone more than a few hours at a time, a crate might not work out well. On other occasions, you may want your dog in the room with you and interacting with you, but you're doing something that could be dangerous for the dog if he got in the middle. (For example, if you like to sew, you don't need a

curious Yorkie puppy "helping" with pinned pieces of fabric that might be laid out on the floor.)

In addition to using a crate, many Yorkie owners on occasion contain their dogs in exercise pens or gated-off areas of the house. Baby gates, available from pet supply stores (and sometimes less expensively from the baby departments of discount stores), can provide a barrier at the door of a kitchen or bathroom, giving a small dog a little bit of freedom while still keeping him out of harm's way. Exercise pens are small, folding, portable wire fences that can be placed anywhere in your home.

Leave your Yorkie in an enclosed area whenever you aren't there to supervise him. Letting a dog, especially a puppy, roam freely throughout the house is a sure recipe for housetraining problems, and this practice needlessly exposes him to numerous household hazards. Before relying on the security of a baby gate or exercise pen, however, watch your dog carefully. Some Yorkies are little climbers and could pull themselves up over baby gates and exercise pens. If your dog is a climber, you'll have to cover the exercise pen, or leave the dog in his crate. A Yorkie could seriously injure himself catapulting off the top of an exercise pen or baby gate.

Identification

Yorkies are clever little dogs who can go flying out the door or squirming through the fence in the blink of an eye. For your dog's safety and your peace of mind, be sure he has identification on him at all times.

Keep an identification tag on your Yorkie's collar with your name and phone number on it. Also, when he is getting his puppy shots, have your dog microchipped. Microchips are rice-sized electronic chips that the vet can inject under your dog's skin. You then register your dog's chip number with its manufacturer. Shelters and veterinarians have scanners to check for microchips if your dog should become lost.

It's possible that not everyone who finds your lost dog has a microchip scanner. However, if you use both ID tags and microchip the odds are excellent that if somehow your beloved little guy gets out of your sight, you will be reunited with each other.

Toys!

Don't forget the "terrier" in Yorkshire Terrier! This breed usually

Think Like a Yorkie

When puppy-proofing your home, try to think of all the potentially dangerous objects and places in your home that would be enticing to a Yorkie. This includes everything from electrical cords to poisonous chemicals that smell or taste appealing to a dog.

Yorkies are portable little dogs who make great travel companions.

loves its toys—especially anything small and squeaky that reminds his little Yorkie heart of a rat.

Puppies need toys that will help with the teething process, and most Yorkies continue to love to play with toys throughout their lifetimes. Different dogs prefer different toys; it's something of a matter of trial and error. Some love plush toys twice their size, while others enjoy tiny tennis balls available at pet supply stores. Still others prefer plastic squeaky toys. Nylabone makes toys that are suitable to a Yorkie's size and chewing power.

Be very careful with any toys that have eyes, threads, or other pieces that can come loose and get stuck in his throat or digestive system. Throw away any stuffing or squeakers if the dog tears the toy apart. Swallowing one of these objects can be a medical emergency! Also, beware of cat toys that have real fur on them. This can be a special, fun, *supervised* toy for your Yorkie, but if you're not there to watch him, your dog's terrier instincts are likely to kick in, resulting in a swallowed fur toy. This will lead to a trip to the emergency room. Never leave your dog alone with a toy that he is likely to shred, because you have no way of knowing if he will swallow pieces of the toy while you aren't there to supervise him.

Many Yorkies love their toys and even collect them, sitting in the middle of their "prizes." Enjoy!

PUPPY-PROOFING YOUR HOME

A Yorkie's cleverness sometimes can get him into serious trouble. These terriers often climb, they almost all love to burrow, they pounce on anything that's dropped, and they worm their way into spaces that are too small for a gnat. This is why it's so important to puppy-proof your home!

Before you bring your puppy home, be sure that electrical cords are covered. (You can get cord covers at computer stores and at many variety stores.) Make sure any dangerous household chemicals are stored in a top cabinet—or better yet, go "green" and try to use only nontoxic, earth-friendly (and Yorkie-friendly!) products.

Get a bottle of bitter apple spray or a similar product from a pet supply store. This is a harmless spray with a very unpleasant taste. Spray it on anything the dog is likely to chew.

Two products don't belong in any Yorkie home: slug bait and traditional, sweet-tasting antifreeze. Slug bait is a horrible,

Get toys for your Yorkie that are appropriate for his small size, and be sure to avoid any that may pose a choking hazard.

lethal concoction that causes the deaths of many dogs every year. Antifreeze is just as awful. A *half teaspoon* (4.9 ml) of antifreeze can kill an adult Yorkie! A number of brands of antifreeze on the market now have bitter tastes and a less lethal set of ingredients.

Put baby gates at the tops of stairs so that curious puppies don't take a step and go tumbling down. Look at what's on low-lying surfaces, such as coffee tables, and remove anything that might conceivably be in the reach of your new dog.

Yorkie puppies are just like human toddlers—they somehow always will make a beeline for the most dangerous thing they can find. Look around your house for items that might pose a danger to your dog, and plan ahead as much as you can.

THE HOMECOMING

You've made all the preparations, and now it's time to bring your new four-footed family member home. This is a wonderful time for you and your new dog! If it's at all possible, you might want to take off at least a week from work to help your new Yorkie adjust to life in his new home.

Bringing Your Yorkie Home

Your Yorkie's trip home should be in a safe, comfy crate filled with some nice bedding and a toy or two. Have multiple towels ready so that you can replace his bedding if he happens to get carsick on the way home.

Be sure the dog goes potty before he gets in your car. If the drive home is a long one, plan to make a potty stop or two along the way. However, if you're traveling with a puppy who hasn't had his full complement of vaccinations, don't let him walk on grass that has been used by strange dogs. This may expose him to deadly parvo and distemper viruses that his system can't handle.

Bonding With Your Yorkie

Plan to spend a couple of quiet days with your new puppy or adult dog. Let him explore your home at his own pace. Don't force yourself on him, and don't invite all your friends over for a look at your new wonder dog. Let him have some time to just get acquainted with you and to adjust to his new home.

Some Yorkies will be wagging their tails with glee within minutes of coming home, but others are more cautious and adjust more slowly. Your bond of trust with your dog will be strengthened by letting him adjust to his new life at his own speed and in his own way. Give him time to rest and relax. Don't poke at him when he's sleeping or try to wake him up to get him to play.

Sleeping With Your Yorkie

Decide ahead of time where your Yorkie is going to sleep. Because dogs are pack animals, they are happiest if they get to spend their sleeping time near their human "pack." Your Yorkie will be a more content, more bonded pet if he sleeps in your room. Place his crate near your bed where he can see you, and let him know that he's part of the family.

Frankly, many—probably most—Yorkie owners sleep with their dogs on their beds, whether they admit it in public or not. It's not like the little guys take up a lot of room. However, if your Yorkie *ever* growls at you, snaps at you, or otherwise shows bullying behavior, he doesn't belong in your bed. Let him sleep in a crate by your bed, but don't give him doggy social status by allowing him to sleep in your space. If your dog is behaving sweetly with you and your family, let him sleep wherever you find most comfortable.

Many Yorkie owners say their best night's sleep is in a bed full of little Yorkies, snuggling through the night.

You can tote your little Yorkie just about anywhere, but be sure to make the proper arrangements for him before traveling.

TRAVEL

Yorkies are portable little dogs who make great travel companions. Use a few precautions, plan ahead, and you and your dog will have years of fun exploring new places together.

In the Car

All too often, you'll see someone in traffic with a little dog sitting on her lap. While this looks adorable, it is a death sentence for your little guy if the airbag deploys. When an airbag goes off, it easily can kill a small child. It also can kill a small dog. If you have front-seat airbags, be sure that your dog *always* travels in the back seat!

By far, the safest form of travel for your little dog is a comfortable crate. A loose pooch in the car is a possible hazard to driving, and your dog is in real danger if you're in a car accident.

Keep a crate in the backseat of your car, securely fastened to the seat belts. When you hop into the car, put your happy traveler in his crate. Think of his crate as the canine equivalent of a kid's car seat. Your dog will travel in comfort, and you'll both have a good time on the trip.

In the Air

Your Yorkie can fly with you in the cabin of most major airlines. If you'll be flying with your dog, purchase specially designed carry-on luggage that you can safely and securely tuck underneath the seat. Several companies make soft-sided, airline-approved carry-on bags for dogs and cats. These bags look very much like any carry-on luggage, except for the netting that gives your pet ventilation. Few other passengers will even notice that you're carrying a dog on board. You can purchase these carriers at pet supply stores or online. (Be sure that the particular bag you select is labeled as meeting airline size requirements.)

Before you fly, get your Yorkie used to getting into, out of, and relaxing in this smaller carrier. Walk around with him in the carrier so that he gets used to the sensation. If he's used to riding in the car in a crate, going in his own personal bag in a plane will be simple and fun for you both.

Airlines charge for pets in the cabin, and most restrict the number of animals per flight to one or two. As soon as you know that you'll be traveling, call the airline and make arrangements for your pet to fly with you. Check with the airline for any additional requirements. You may need to have a current health certificate for your dog, which you can get from your veterinarian.

Many small dogs cross the country—and even the oceans—every day. Most of these frequent flyers take the trip happily in stride.

Traveling Without Your Yorkie

You can't always take your Yorkie with you when you travel, and the odds are you'll need to board him from time to time. To make this a hassle-free experience, you'll need to plan well ahead of time—don't make this a last-minute decision.

Boarding Your Yorkie

Here are some tips in selecting a boarding facility for your Yorkie:

- Ask for recommendations from your breeder, your veterinarian, and your groomer. Word of mouth means a lot in this business.

- Go for an unannounced visit during regular business hours. Get a feel for the place and a feel for the person who potentially will care for your pet. Even an older facility should be gleaming with cleanliness, and it should smell fresh. If a lingering odor is present, something is wrong. The facility also should feel happy. Look to see if animals seem reasonably relaxed and unafraid. If you don't get a good feel for the place, don't leave your pet there.

- Ask what services the kennel provides. Will your Yorkie have one-on-one time with a person who pets him and grooms him? Will he have a comfy bed, or do they just put blankets out on a cement floor? Some facilities charge extra for playtime, grooming, giving medication, and even feeding your pet his own food. Others include these as part of a blanket price. Be sure you know what services your pet will receive for the amount you're paying.

If you have to leave your Yorkie behind when traveling, you can board him or hire a pet sitter to take care of him in your home.

- Pay attention to what questions the boarding facility staff asks you. They should care a lot about your dog—his patterns, his favorite activities, what cheers him up, and what you want to do in case of a medical emergency.

In-Home Pet Sitters

Pet sitters come to your home two or more times a day, and some even spend the night. They can take care of your dog in the familiarity of his own home. That may be a better alternative than the stress of a kennel, especially if you have a shy or aggressive dog. Ask for references, and spend time

A dog with identification is much more likely to return home if lost than one without it.

getting to know the pet sitter before you travel. Remember that you are trusting this person with the keys to your home while you're away.

In today's world, most people work outside the home. Your Yorkie might need some attention if you work long hours, and a pet sitter might be a good solution. It's not fair for your dog to have to live in a crate 8 or 12 hours a day with no stimulation, no potty breaks, and no human contact. Fortunately, a pet sitter can come in once a day (more often if needed) and entertain your Yorkie for a half hour. Services vary, but they might include a potty break and playtime, a walk, or even a playtime with a pre-approved, compatible small dog.

Find a pet sitter near you by asking for recommendations from your veterinarian and groomer, or look online. Of course, check out the pet sitter you choose carefully! You are trusting this person with your dog and giving her access to your home. Most of the people in this business love animals so much that they are truly kind and

wonderful, but a bit of caution is always in order.

Doggy Day Care

During the last several years, doggy day cares have sprung up around the country. Nowadays, almost as many day cares exist for "fur kids" as for human kids. This can be a great option for your Yorkie *if* you have a social dog who loves to hang out with other animals. Spend time at the day care and see if it looks like a safe place for a small dog. Some day cares have separate areas for large dogs and small ones, which is a very, very wise idea. Don't take your small dog to a place where large dogs are allowed to jump and paw at your little one—it can be a dangerous situation.

A well-organized, well-supervised doggy day care that understands the needs of small dogs can be a great option for a Yorkie with working "parents."

THE LOST DOG

Few experiences are scarier than realizing that your dog is gone. Don't panic, but do act right away. Every minute you lose makes it harder to get your dog home.

What to Do

The following are some crucial steps to take if your dog becomes lost:

- Don't wait to act. Contact your neighbors and tell them your Yorkie is missing. Talk especially with neighborhood children, people walking their dogs, and anyone else who spends time in the area.
- Call your local animal shelter and report that your Yorkie is missing. Go personally every day to see if your dog is there. Check shelters in nearby towns. Ask the shelter staff if private animal rescue groups might be caring for your animal. Do not

Keeping Calm in a Crisis

If your dog becomes lost, the most important thing you can do is not panic. Act quickly: Contact neighbors and animal shelters, put up fliers, and of course search for him yourself, but panicking will not help and actually may hurt your attempts to recover your dog.

give up checking the shelters, and do not think a phone call will do. You would be amazed at what breed of dog someone will label an incoming animal at the shelter. If the staff thinks your dog is a Cairn Terrier, and you call and ask if a Yorkie is there, they will tell you no.

- Create a flyer with a photo of your dog. Include the dog's name, sex, color, age, and identifying marks (or tags). Offer a reward. Post the flyer everywhere: schools, banks, grocery stores, animal shelters, gas stations, coffee houses, and anywhere that will allow them.
- Call every animal-related business in your area: veterinarians, groomers, doggy day cares, pet boutiques, and obedience trainers. Let them know that you have a missing Yorkie. Make sure they take your number, and post your flyer at their business.
- Call your breeder. A word-of-mouth network exists among breeders that sometimes will help you find your missing pet.
- Ask your breeder, shelter, or local kennel club for a contact in

Yorkie rescue. Sometimes people take an animal to breed rescue without checking with a local shelter.
- Advertise in the newspaper.
- Advertise on the radio.
- Don't give up. Sometimes people keep a dog for days, weeks, or months before they see a poster or sign or decide to take the animal to a shelter.

Identification: The Fastest Road Home

Dogs with identification are much more likely to make it home than dogs without it. Keep a tag on your dog at all times with your phone number on it. Most people will call when they see the tag.

Microchipping your Yorkie is also a good idea, because it is a simple, inexpensive, and effective way to find your pet. As mentioned earlier, a microchip is a tiny, rice-sized chip that veterinarians and shelters can scan. Each chip has a unique number. The veterinarian or shelter can call this number into the microchip company, and you will be reunited with your dog in a matter of minutes. One caution, though: Be sure to keep your phone number and contact information up to date with the microchip company. The microchip doesn't do your pet any good if the listed phone numbers are no longer where you can be reached.

Your little dog will be your best friend for more than the next decade of your life. Think carefully when you select him, and give him the best care possible when you bring him home. You'll never regret investing the time and effort into giving your best friend a great start in his life with you.

FEEDING
Your Yorkshire Terrier

Your little dog eats tiny amounts, and it's important that every little mouthful is packed with nutrition to keep him healthy and long lived. This chapter will help you make the right decisions for you and your little guy.

In today's nutrition-conscious world, everyone seems to be a self-appointed authority on exactly what you should feed your Yorkie. They will tell you if you don't follow their advice, you're being an irresponsible, uncaring dog owner.

Unfortunately, the self-appointed experts—and even the honest-to-goodness experts—seem to disagree more and more by the day. It can be overwhelming to people who just want to take care of the dog they love.

Remember, Yorkies usually live long, healthy lives, and they seem to thrive no matter what we do. A lot of good choices are available for you that that will certainly help your dog look and feel his best throughout that long lifetime.

WHEN TO FEED

From the time a puppy is weaned from his mother's milk until he's three months old, he must be fed four times a day. From three months until six months, feed him three times a day. After age six months, feed him twice a day. Meals should be spaced evenly throughout the day, but the last meal should be at least three hours before bedtime so that you don't have nighttime housetraining problems.

People who are accustomed to feeding adult dogs just once a day are surprised by the recommendation to feed twice daily. Most veterinarians now think it's a good idea for all breeds, and especially for very small and very large dogs. Yorkies have small digestive systems, and they're likely to better digest and absorb their food if they have two small meals instead of one large one. Yorkies are also prone to hypoglycemia, so having two meals helps to keep blood sugar levels more even throughout the day.

HOW MUCH TO FEED

If you've always known that your friend could eat twice as much as you could and still stay skinny, life with dogs proves your experience was true. The amount of food a dog needs depends on many things, including his size, his age, his energy level, and the amount of exercise he gets every day. It also depends on his metabolism (just like you and your friend).

Ask your dog's breeder how much food the dog has been getting at each meal. Make sure she's specific! If the dog starts to gain weight, slightly reduce his portion. If he begins looking a little too thin, slightly increase it. Remember, a Yorkie is a tiny dog. He doesn't eat very much. The biggest mistake most people make is overfeeding a Yorkie, not underfeeding him.

Scheduled Feeding

Feed your Yorkie regular, scheduled meals—don't just leave a dish down on the floor all day for your dog to snack from. This can make a positive, important difference in the life of your little dog. Feeding your Yorkie regular meals is a good idea because:

- You will know when your dog is sick. The fastest way to notice a health problem is when your dog eats less at his meals for a day or two. No matter how observant you are, you can't catch this as quickly if you free-feed. Noticing a dog or puppy is "off his feed" on the first day can make the difference between life and death in some cases.
- You will have a better relationship with your dog. Your Yorkie may not look like a wolf, but he shares his wolf ancestor's view of who runs the pack. When your dog chooses when and where he eats, he assumes he's in charge of the house. When you give your dog regular meals, he assumes you're in charge of the house.
- The difference in your dog's behavior when you switch from free-feeding to giving your dog scheduled meals can be almost magical. Shy dogs will get more confident and pushy dogs will become gentler, because you have established yourself as the leader of the pack.
- It will help with housetraining your Yorkie. A regular schedule for input means a regular schedule for output. You'll know when to watch for signs to take him outside.
- Feeding your Yorkie regular meals will help you control his portions better, which in turn allows you to control your dog's weight—the key to a long and healthy life.

The Finicky Eater

While most Yorkies gobble their meals, some pick at them. They look at their food, give you that sad and soulful look, and walk away. Or they lie down and stare at it, as if they are so disappointed

Will Work for Food

Always ask your dog to work for his dinner and treats. You work hard to earn the money to feed him—he can work to earn his keep! Ask him to sit or do a trick before you feed him. This reinforces that you are the benevolent and gentle yet powerful leader who controls the food in the house.

Remember, you still should be feeding your dog the same great food and healthy treats you did before. You're just asking him to cooperate to get his reward. He will be a calmer, better-adjusted pet because he will know he has a human who is acting like a leader.

Asking your dog to sit or perform a trick before you feed him will reinforce your status as a gentle leader.

you didn't do a better job. Some turn up their noses until their human "mom" brings them something much more palatable—say, her dinner!

Picky eaters tend to be underweight, which will be a huge problem if your little Yorkie ever has any health problems. Worse yet, they aren't getting proper nutrition from their food, which is bad for their immune systems.

Assuming your dog is healthy, the answer is to stick with your meal plan. Put his meal in front of him. If he doesn't eat it in about 20 minutes, take it away and don't feed him anything until his next scheduled meal. Mix up fresh food for his next meal, put it in front of him, and then take it away if he doesn't eat. By the third mealtime, your dog will eat his food, and he likely will turn into a hearty eater.

While most dogs can skip two meals without worry, talk with your veterinarian before trying this technique with an underweight dog. Puppies shouldn't skip meals, and dogs with hypoglycemia mustn't skip any meals. Your dog's finicky eating may be a symptom that he's sick. With these cautions in mind, kindly but firmly putting your dog on a feeding schedule almost always will cure a finicky eater, as long as the dog is healthy.

WHERE TO FEED

The best place to feed your dog is in his crate. This gives him a safe, quiet place to enjoy his meals. It also gives your dog a positive association with his crate.

Picking the Right Food

Yorkies are especially prone to dental problems, so kibble may be the best choice of food for your dog, as its crunchy texture helps to remove tartar from his teeth. If your Yorkie is a particularly finicky eater, you may be able to mix a bit of canned food in with the kibble to improve the taste.

Feed your Yorkie a high-quality food for optimal nutritional benefits.

If you have more than one dog, make sure each one has his own dish at mealtimes and that no one can steal anyone else's food. This is a surefire way to create animosity between your dogs, and you won't be able to track how well each of them is eating. Don't allow mealtimes to become stressful events. Give each animal a safe place to finish an uninterrupted meal.

WHAT TO FEED

It's extremely important to feed your Yorkie high-quality food. Depending on your little guy's size and metabolism, he could be eating less than 1/2 cup (118.3 ml) of food a day. Even a few mouthfuls of doggy "junk food" can have a serious impact on your dog's nutrition. Feeding your dog the right food in the right amounts is one of the best things you can do for your Yorkie.

This doesn't seem too complicated until you find yourself trying to pick out dog food at a major pet supply store. You'll find yourself staring at more than 150 brands, varieties, and flavors of dog food. Add to this all of the contradictory advice from people about what's best for your dog, and it's enough to make you want to throw up your hands in frustration. Once you break down the choices available to you, however, the right food for your Yorkie will become a lot clearer. You'll be able to decide on something that

Feeding dry food will keep your Yorkie's teeth free of tartar.

works for you and your pet.

Before you worry about areas in which knowledgeable people disagree, let's talk about the area in which everyone agrees: Quality counts! The better the quality of ingredients that go into your Yorkie's food, the better it will be for your dog.

Whatever decisions you make regarding what to feed your Yorkie, keep a careful eye on him. Is his coat shiny and silky? Is his skin supple? Is he free of itching and dryness? Are his eyes free of watering or discharge? Are his stools firm? If your dog looks exceptionally healthy, then the diet you have chosen is most likely the right one for him. If he doesn't look quite as wonderful as he might, it's time to consider some of the alternatives that are available to you.

Commercial Dog Foods

The vast majority of Yorkie owners feed their dogs some form of commercial dog food. The Association of American Feed Control Officials (AAFCO) sets standards that most pet foods meet, ensuring that the food contains the right mix of such things as protein, fats, and vitamins. Although these standards are a good place to start, they don't guarantee that the products used in the food actually will deliver those nutrients to your pet.

Yorkies don't eat a lot of food, so there's no reason not to spend a little extra money and get a premium brand for your dog. These foods may not be available in grocery stores; look for them at pet supply stores or at your veterinarian's office. Before you buy, read the ingredients listed on the package.

Be wary of dog foods that provide most of their protein through meat and chicken by-products or meal—the real deal of plain old "chicken" or "beef" is better. Compare labels, and you'll see that the premium brands have meat as the first few ingredients rather than soy, wheat, corn, or beet pulp.

Dry Food

If you're feeding your Yorkie a commercial diet, it's important to feed kibble as his primary source of food. Yorkies, like other toy breeds, have dental problems. Although feeding kibble by no means solves the problem of Yorkie tooth loss, it will help somewhat to keep tartar accumulation under control.

In addition to having good-quality ingredients, the kibble should be comfortable for your dog to eat. Kibble that's sized to be crunchy for a Golden Retriever might actually be bigger than your Yorkie's mouth! Several companies have brands that are designed to be easily chewed by small dogs, and they feature kibble shapes that are easier for little guys to pick up.

When you bring kibble home, open the bag and smell the food. It should smell like a fresh biscuit, not musty or rancid. If you have just one or two dogs, get the smallest sized bags of food, and purchase new food if the kibble loses its fresh smell.

Semi-Moist and Canned Food

There are several brands of semi-moist food on the market. The disadvantage to feeding semi-moist food or canned food as the primary part of your dog's diet is that soft foods can hasten dental problems. There isn't anything scraping against the teeth, so tartar buildup is more likely. If you feed semi-moist or canned food, be sure to brush your dog's teeth regularly, and give him toys to chew on that will help reduce tartar buildup.

As with dry food, look carefully at the ingredients and choose a food with the best possible nutritional value for your pet. Beware

Quality Food for a Quality Dog

Purchase a premium brand of food for your Yorkie to guarantee that he's eating the best ingredients and receiving ideal nutrition. Your veterinarian can recommend a good-quality food for your pet.

Starting Out With Your New Puppy

A puppy should stay on the food his breeder was feeding him for at least a week before starting any transitions. He doesn't need an upset tummy in addition to his other adjustments to his new home!

Be sure that:

- You have your puppy's food on hand before he comes home.
- The breeder has told you how often and when he eats. (Keep him on the same schedule for the first week.)
- The breeder has told you how much he eats.

Make any changes to your puppy's food gradually after the first week, mixing a little of the new food in with the old, slowly increasing the percentage of new food over the course of several days.

Most veterinarians recommend feeding a premium-quality food formulated specifically for puppies during the first year.

of the fact that some of the semi-moist foods contain a lot of preservatives.

Chemical-Free Commercial Foods

Historically, most pet foods have added the chemical preservatives BHA, BHT, or ethoxyquin to extend the product's shelf life. These additives have been a bone of considerable contention, because of concern that they can cause cancer.

Natural alternatives to chemical preservatives are available. In fact, many dog foods are now preserved with "mixed tocopherols" (vitamin E). Seeing consumers' preferences for naturally preserved food, even major pet food brands are increasingly turning to natural preservatives.

Because Yorkie tummies are tiny, and because natural preservatives don't last as long as chemical ones, keep a close eye (and a sharp nose) focused on your dry dog food packages. If the food seems less fresh toward the end of the bag, go ahead and buy a fresh bag and discard the old one.

Today, there is a major trend toward more natural, wholesome dog foods. Many now only use ingredients that pass federal inspections for human food. (They will say something like "human grade" or "USDA-inspected meats" on the packaging.) Some dog food brands now contain certified organic ingredients. These more wholesome brands are available at the growing number of pet health food stores, through mail order, online, and at some pet supply stores. In fact, some major healthy food grocery store chains now stock several brands of premium, all-natural dog food.

Your Yorkie always should have access to plenty of fresh water.

Going natural isn't cheap. However, for many Yorkie lovers, the security of knowing the quality of ingredients is worth the extra cost. Because your Yorkie doesn't eat a lot, it won't add a lot to your budget to feed him the best.

Home-Cooked Meals

Given the benefit of fresh, healthy ingredients, an increasing number of Yorkshire Terrier owners are cooking their own dog food. Although home-cooked meals can be very beneficial to your dog, if you don't do it right, home cooking can do far more harm than good.

Dogs have different needs in terms of the mix of carbohydrates, proteins, and fats in their diets than humans. Therefore, it's important to talk with your veterinarian before considering cooking for your pet.

A number of doggy cookbooks are out there on the bookstore shelves. Some of them have wonderful meal plans for your dog, but others are only a recipe for disaster and don't provide the nutrients to keep your dog healthy.

Before you begin to cook for your dog, talk with your

veterinarian. Ask her to take a look at the diets that you're thinking of trying to make sure the meal plans will meet your Yorkie's nutritional needs.

Raw Foods

Over the past several years, a raw foods diet revolution has emerged in the world of pet care. Those who feed their dogs raw foods swear by the results. While skeptics worry about threats of salmonella and E. coli, those who advocate the diet respond that a dog's digestive tract is designed to handle raw meat.

It is extremely important to do research before putting your dog on a homemade raw food diet. Correctly done, this diet of raw meat and pulverized vegetables will provide the correct balance of nutrients and enzymes that your dog needs to be healthy. Feeding your dog raw meat alone will result in an undernourished, sick dog in short order. Several books give instructions for preparing raw foods for your dog.

Many companies make frozen raw-food diets, which should be kept in your freezer until thawing shortly before your dog's meal. These meals meet the AAFCO's nutrition requirements, so you know that your dog is getting everything he needs in his food. They are much more expensive than other kinds of food, but again, because Yorkies eat little, the cost of switching to these foods is minimal. Look for a brand that has small cubes or medallions that can translate into Yorkie-size meals, rather than having to defrost larger loaves (or experiencing the frustration of trying to chip away a meal from a frozen loaf).

If you feed raw food, scrupulously follow a hygiene regimen of only feeding freshly defrosted food, washing food bowls thoroughly with soap and water, and washing your hands carefully after handling the food. Never leave the dog's food out for more than about 15 to 20 minutes; discard the food if he doesn't eat it by that time.

The next few years should produce more information that will tell us whether raw food diets are just a fad or a major revolution that will improve the health of dogs.

Prescription Diets

Only your veterinarian can determine the best prescription diet for a dog who has medical issues. Amazingly, in today's Internet age,

Vet Advice

If you want to cook your dog home-made meals or prepare your own raw diet, talk with your veterinarian. If you are committed to this kind of feeding and your veterinarian isn't supportive, find a veterinarian who has a holistic practice and who has the expertise to support your feeding decisions and provide knowledgeable advice.

Make all changes to your dog's diet gradually. If you're changing from one brand of food to another, gradually add a little of the new food to the old, taking a week to finally transition to the new brand.

people are asking for diet advice from perfect strangers who have never met their dogs, rather than talking with their veterinarians. The Internet can be a good source of general information, and it can give you good questions to ask your veterinarian, but nothing replaces a veterinarian's knowledge of your dog.

Your veterinarian may suggest a prescription diet if your dog has a chronic health problem. For example, dogs with kidney or liver disease generally benefit from a low-protein diet. If your dog suffers from allergies, your veterinarian may recommend an elimination diet in which the dog only has a couple of ingredients in his meals. Gradually, additional ingredients are added one at a time, so that the veterinarian can identify what foods trigger your dog's allergies. Sometimes, the original elimination diet includes food the dog has never eaten before, such as duck, venison, or even kangaroo meat.

A number of dog food companies now make a wide variety of prescription diets. In some cases, your veterinarian may give you directions for making home-cooked meals for your dog.

Supplements

Don't give your dog any vitamins without discussing them with your veterinarian. Some vitamins are toxic at high levels. However, a variety of additives that people give their Yorkies can be beneficial. Omega-3 fatty acids from fish oil can aid digestion, improve coat, and help with allergies. Evidence suggests that glucosamine and chondroitin sulfate can keep joints healthy. If you want to add items such as these to your dog's diet, discuss them with your veterinarian to be sure you're not overdoing them.

Bones

Do not ever give your Yorkie a cooked bone of any kind. Any cooked bone can be deadly, but chicken and turkey bones are especially dangerous. The process of cooking a bone (even just for a few minutes) makes the bone brittle. The bone will turn into sharp little shards that can rip through your Yorkie's stomach and intestines. If your dog accidentally gets access to a cooked bone and eats it, call your veterinarian right away.

On the other hand, raw bones can be very healthy for your dog. Chewing on a raw bone will help keep your dog's teeth healthy and strong. While you always should supervise your dog when he is eating a bone, a raw bone isn't likely to splinter like a cooked one does. Always be sure the bone is large enough so that the dog can't get it lodged in his throat.

Treats

Dogs are healthiest when they're eating a well-balanced diet, whether it's a commercially prepared kibble, a home-cooked meal, or a carefully planned and prepared raw food regimen. Don't upset your dog's balanced diet with lots of needless treats.

Of course, modern obedience training is based on the joys of working for food. You don't have to turn your Yorkie into a tank to train him, though! It's important to remember that a tiny amount of food goes a long way with a little dog. With this in mind, training rewards should be no larger than the size of a pencil eraser.

Use good-quality treats when you train, such as string cheese or tiny pieces of cooked meat. (Don't use hot dogs or other foods full of salt and chemicals.) Your Yorkie also will probably love veggies, such as little bits of carrots or tomatoes.

FOODS TO AVOID

Here is a partial list of foods that can make your dog seriously ill—and in some cases even can lead to his death. Remember, because your dog is small, just a tiny amount of very toxic things might be lethal to your dog. It's always better to be overly cautious rather than not cautious enough.

Alcoholic Beverages

Yorkies are tiny dogs, and a very small amount of alcohol can cause alcohol poisoning.

Avocados

A toxic component called "persin" is the culprit. Dogs have died from eating avocados, but the toxic dose isn't yet known. It's best to avoid letting your pet eat an avocado.

Chocolate

The darker chocolates are the most dangerous, but even milk chocolate can make your dog sick. Cocoa mulch is popular with some gardeners, but it is poisonous if a dog ingests it.

ASPCA Animal Poison Control Center

To learn more about toxic foods and other substances, go to the ASPCA Animal Poison Control Center's website (www.aspca.org).

If your Yorkie has eaten something that might be toxic, call your veterinarian or emergency clinic right away. You also can call the ASPCA Animal Poison Control Center, which is staffed 24 hours a day, 365 days a year. It charges a fee for a consultation, but the staff are true experts in the field. Their toll-free number is (888) 426-4435.

Dogs are at their healthiest when they're eating a well-balanced diet.

Coffee

Coffee includes your latte, the coffee beans, and the coffee grounds. Caffeine can give your dog serious heart and neurological problems.

Grapes and Raisins

These seemingly healthful snacks have recently been proven to cause kidney failure in some dogs. Keep them away from your dog. If he eats some, contact your veterinarian right away—it might be a medical emergency.

Macadamia Nuts

As few as six nuts have caused severe toxic reactions in dogs. The mechanism for the problem isn't yet known.

Moldy Food

Some molds cause a neurological problem in some dogs.

Onions

Dogs don't have the enzyme needed to digest onions, so eating them can lead to severe gastrointestinal distress. Large amounts of onions can cause your dog to become anemic. Garlic can have the same effect, but dogs rarely eat enough garlic to cause a substantial problem.

Yeast Dough

When your dog eats raw dough, it will "rise" in his stomach, dangerously stretching and expanding it. Alcohol is also produced when the dough "rises," and this can create alcohol poisoning in your Yorkie.

PORTLY YORKIES

While many Yorkies stay naturally thin, some tend to become pudgy in the blink of an eye. It's incredibly important to keep your little guy slender. Here are a few reasons why:

- Your dog will live longer. One study shows that slender dogs live almost two years longer than dogs who eat more. (See box on "The Importance of Being Slender.")
- Weight makes other conditions worse. For example, if your Yorkie has a collapsing trachea, a condition in which the windpipe narrows and folds on itself, extra weight puts even more stress on the dog's trachea and can shorten his life. If he has conditions such as heart disease, kidney problems, or liver disease, all of those organs have to work harder if he's carrying some extra ounces.
- Recent research indicates that substances in fat are actually inflammatories. They cause joints to hurt more—in addition to the extra weight the animal is carrying. Your dog will feel less pain as he ages if he's slender.
- Your slender dog will want to play more, go for more walks, and have more fun. These magical creatures are here on earth for such a short time, it's important to make every day feel good by keeping them thin.

The Body Beautiful

When your Yorkie is at his ideal weight, you will be able to feel the outline of his ribs under your fingers. He'll have a definite waist when you view him from above. He'll also have a tuck-up on his tummy between his ribs and hips. If he's overweight, you won't see a definite waist. You'll have to poke through a layer of fat to find those ribs, and his belly will be rounded when you look at him from the side.

You love your dog no matter how he looks, of course. But if you want to have him in your life for as many as two extra years, you need to be sure his body is slender.

Losing Weight

Most likely, if you watch your Yorkie's snacks and add a little exercise to his day, he'll lose the weight he needs to. If that isn't enough, develop a diet with his doctor.

Your doctor probably will suggest reducing the portions of his

The Importance of Being Slender

In a study conducted by Purina, a group of 48 Labrador Retrievers were followed for their lifetimes. Half were allowed to eat as much as they wanted, and the other half were fed 25 percent less. The differences were startling.

The median life span of the lean-fed dogs was extended by 15 percent, or nearly two years—11.2 years for the control group versus 13 years for the lean-fed dogs. By age ten, only three lean-fed dogs had died, compared to seven control group dogs. At the end of the twelfth year, 11 lean-fed dogs were alive, compared with only 1 control dog who was still alive. Twenty-five percent of the lean-fed group survived to 13.5 years, while none of the control group dogs lived to 13.5 years.

In addition, according to observations of the researchers, the control dogs exhibited more visible signs of aging, such as graying muzzles, impaired gaits, and reduced activity, at an earlier age than the lean-fed dogs.

The bottom line is that how much a dog eats—and that includes your Yorkie—matters. You will have your dog longer, and he will feel better during those years if you keep him slender.

regular food rather than putting him on some sort of diet food. She might suggest that you add some low-calorie goodies to his food such as green beans or pumpkin to keep up the volume while reducing the amount of calories.

Also, when giving your Yorkie treats, you may want to switch to more healthful snacks, such as pieces of carrots.

When Your Seemingly Portly Yorkie Isn't Really Fat

At times, your dog may seem fat, but instead he is really showing signs of a different problem. Dogs with low thyroid levels gain weight, and diets don't help. Once your dog is diagnosed with the problem, he can receive medication and go back to his slender self.

A swollen abdomen may look like a fat dog, but you'll realize that your dog has a round tummy but slender shoulders and hips. A swollen tummy is always an indication to see your veterinarian as soon as possible. It may be something as simple as a case of puppy worms that needs to be treated. On the other hand, the condition can be as devastating as fluids accumulating in your dog's abdomen—a sign of life-threatening health problems that need immediate attention.

If your dog seems to have gained weight in a short period of time and has a distended tummy, call your veterinarian right away.

FEEDING YOUR SENIOR YORKIE

When your Yorkie is about seven or so, have a talk with his doctor about his senior years. Your veterinarian may want to run a

Fatty Foods

Yorkies are one of the breeds with a higher than average incidence of pancreatitis—a potentially fatal inflammation of the pancreas. Rich foods, such as fatty meats and gravy, can trigger an attack that can land your Yorkie in the emergency veterinary clinic. It's important to never feed your dog foods such as turkey skin, Thanksgiving gravy, and other rich foods that can create a problem.

series of senior wellness checks on him.

As long as your senior is a healthy dog, your veterinarian probably will recommend that you keep feeding him the same food he's been getting. It used to be believed that older dogs needed lower protein foods, but that has now generally been discounted, unless the dog has specific health concerns that would benefit from a low-protein regimen.

Many Yorkies, like other toy dogs, have lost many teeth by the time they reach their senior years. Consequently, make sure your dog can comfortably eat what you are feeding him. You may want to feed him smaller-sized kibbles or moisten his food.

Keeping your Yorkie at his ideal weight will help him live a longer and healthier life.

Sometimes older dogs get to be finicky eaters. To entice him to eat, try warming moist foods a bit in the microwave. You can add just a smidge of healthy food such as lean meat (or the meat in baby food). Sometimes, three smaller meals a day work better than two for the oldsters.

It's very important for your Yorkie to eat a well-balanced, nutritious diet. Always purchase the best-quality food that you can for your little dog. Yorkies don't eat a lot of food, so it won't cost you much more to feed your dog the very best food available. Let your dog eat (properly) and be merry—the proper diet will allow you and your dog to share many happy years together.

Chapter

GROOMING
Your Yorkshire Terrier

h, hair. A Yorkie's most notable feature is his glorious hair. A well-groomed Yorkie shimmers and shines. His coat is more like the glow of gold and steel than dog fur.

All of this takes a lot of work.

Even if, like most Yorkie owners, you decide to keep your pet in a comfy, clipped-down coif, keeping your dog groomed is still a considerable commitment of time and effort. While coat care is an obvious concern when you groom your Yorkie, other things must be considered as well. His teeth need to be brushed, his ears and eyes need to be cleaned, and his little toenails need regular trimming.

PREPARING YOUR YORKIE TO LOVE GROOMING

Grooming is a major part of a Yorkie's life. Even if he's trimmed into a shorter pet clip, he'll need combing at least three times a week; many Yorkies need to be combed every day. If he's in a longer clip, you'll be committed to a regime of extensive daily brushing, rolling hair into wraps, and pulling topknots into rubber bands. Add to that the regular teeth cleaning, nail trimming, and general maintenance any dog needs, and your dog is spending a lot of his little life being groomed.

If he sees this as torture, he's going to spend a lot of unhappy hours—and an unhappy Yorkie is no fun to groom. It's your job to help your dog to think that grooming is a happy experience. How do you do this? By pairing grooming behaviors with happy, tail-wagging times with your pet.

Teach "Lift Up"

Yorkie grooming should happen on your lap, in a sink, or on a table. That means that your dog has to be lifted into the air to be groomed. Much of the conflict that people experience in grooming their Yorkies comes from dogs who hate to be picked up. You can reduce your dog's stress—and therefore your stress—by teaching your Yorkie the "lift up" command.

Think how scary it must be for your little dog to be lifted off the ground. Compared

Pet Yorkies can be clipped in a style called the "puppy clip," which features medium-length hair all over the body.

to your little Yorkie, you're about the size of a five-story building. All your dog knows is that sometimes a huge hand comes flying out of the air, picks him up, and does strange things to him. Of course he doesn't like it.

You can teach him to tolerate it, and even like it, by letting him know what is going on. Every day, pick up your dog with a cue word such as "lift up" (or "uppers" or "up, up, up"—whatever feels natural for you to say). Be sure to hold his body comfortably, supporting his chest and rear. Picking him up around the ribs or having his back legs dangling in the air can be extremely uncomfortable for your dog. When you've picked him up, tell him, "Good dog!" and give him a treat. Repeat this frequently, and soon he'll welcome being picked up.

Teach Your Dog the Names of His Body Parts

Imagine someone grabbing at your personal parts without even warning you. You'd probably consider biting anyone who did that to you. However, you're able to accept touching from your doctor or having your hairdresser pull your hair because you know what's coming next. In the same way, a dog who knows the names of his body parts will be much calmer when he's being groomed because he'll be able to anticipate what you're about to do next. (This technique is also very helpful at the veterinarian's office.)

When you touch your dog, give him treats, saying, "Good nose!" or "Good feet!" Over time, he'll associate being touched—even in delicate areas—with a happy experience. Teach him names for his eyes, ears, feet, nose, tail, teeth, tummy, and rear end.

Next, pair the phrase with a gentle touch and a quick food

reward. For example, just touch his toes gently, saying, "Good feet!" and give him a favorite treat. As he's comfortable with his body parts being touched lightly, make the exam more probing, as it would be when he's being groomed or is at the veterinarian. For example, after your dog calmly accepts having his feet touched lightly, begin to gently examine between the pads of his feet. After he's accepted having his muzzle touched, begin to look at his front teeth, and later his back teeth.

Always make this touching fun. It's a happy time between the two of you. Ask other people to touch your dog as well, and have them give your dog a treat. A dog who welcomes touch will find all the grooming demands that a Yorkie goes through as a "day at the spa" rather than some sort of torture devised by unpredictable humans.

THE YORKIE 'DOS

As a Yorkie owner, you can choose among a variety of coat styles, including the show coat, Schnauzer clip, and puppy clip.

Show Coat

Show Yorkies have glamorous coats that are so long they trail on the ground, like the train on a bridal gown. Show exhibitors worry about every single hair, and they carefully protect the coat from breaking. Other than trimming a bit around the feet and possibly trimming at the very end of the coat so that the dog doesn't have trouble moving freely, the dog's hair is kept long and luxurious.

Some people keep their pet Yorkies in full show coat, but it's rare. Doing all the combing, wrapping, and cleaning is a lot of work. In fact, most show exhibitors trim their Yorkies down to a pet clip once the dog's show career is over. It's easier on the dog and the human not to have to constantly fuss with all that hair.

Schnauzer and Puppy Clips

Pet Yorkies (and retired show dogs) are usually trimmed into either a Schnauzer clip or a puppy (also called a layered) clip. In the Schnauzer clip, the dog's hair is shaved short on his back and tummy and left medium length on the legs. The puppy clip looks more like your Yorkie did as a puppy, with medium-length hair all over. With either style, the face is traditionally trimmed in two different ways. One is the modified Westie cut, in which the facial

Grooming Supplies

Grooming your Yorkie will be much easier if you collect your supplies ahead of time rather than fumbling around with a wriggling, wet dog under your arm. Have on hand:

- Nail clippers
- Pin brush
- Comb
- Scissors to trim feet and tidy up coat
- Nonskid mat for sink
- Shampoo
- Conditioner
- Towels
- Hair dryer

hairs are trimmed around the face in a cute, round frame. The other trim leaves longer hair on the top so that your Yorkie can have the traditional topknot topped off with a bow.

Either of these clips keeps your dog looking attractive, feeling comfortable, and relatively easy to care for. Depending on your dog, you'll have to go in to the groomer for a trim about every two or three months. Most people take their dogs to a groomer for trimming, but if you like the idea of doing it yourself, go ahead and try it. You can find detailed instructions online for clipping your Yorkie, and as some sites point out, if you make a mistake, your dog's hair will grow back!

COAT CARE

Your Yorkie needs your help.

Yorkie hair mats easily, and mats hurt! When your Yorkie has a mat on his tummy, it hurts to stretch out and sleep. If your dog has mats on his legs, it hurts to walk. Without question, life is a nightmare for a dog with mats. Human touch can be painful, and your Yorkie might even start snapping at you because he's in constant misery. You need to keep your dog combed, bathed, and trimmed so that he doesn't live this way.

That Amazing Yorkie Coat

Yorkie hair is very much like human hair. There is no undercoat (that fuzzy hair that most breeds have that sheds every spring and fall). The hair grows continuously, just like human hair does. This means that your dog's coat needs daily attention. While more work is involved if you keep a long coat on your Yorkie, even a short 'do requires regular combing and shampooing. Remember that your dog is running, playing, digging, and going for walks in that hair. Of course it will need daily attention.

Begin a grooming routine with your puppy as soon as he comes to your home. It takes several months for a Yorkie coat to achieve a long, flowing look, so use those months wisely. Brush and comb your puppy over every inch of his body. There won't be much hair to comb—and that's just what you want. If your pup gets used to combs and brushes before his coat gets long and likely to mat, he'll think grooming time is a delightful experience. It will never occur to him that it's a struggle.

First, get out a soft brush and brush your puppy all over: his tummy, his feet, his tail, and his head. Then, wipe his face with a washcloth. Give him treats, praise, and tell him he's a little puppy genius. If you do this now, your life will be incomparably easier in the years ahead.

Brushing and Combing Your Yorkie

Your dog's hair will start changing from puppy fluffiness to a bit of length at about four months of age. By the time your dog is 6 months old, his hair will be noticeably longer, and at 12 months of age, he'll have that flowing look. The coats that trail on the ground take at least a couple of years to gain that length, and they require a regimen of committed grooming.

Whatever length your dog's coat is, brush and comb him at least three times a week (daily if he isn't in a short trim). Some Yorkies, even in a short trim, need combing every day. Also, don't ever brush or comb your dog's dry coat. It will break his hair. Spritz his hair with a conditioning spray first and then brush him.

Start with a pin brush and gently brush your dog's entire body. Don't just brush the back and sides; gently brush your dog's tummy, the insides of his legs, and under his tail. It's those hidden places that are likely to develop the worst mats if you're not careful. If your Yorkie has a long coat, brush one section at a time. Be sure you work clear down to the skin, and don't just brush on top of the hair.

Gentleness is the key. If you want your dog to like grooming, you can't jerk and tug. Be thorough and work through every hair on your dog, but do it gently, lovingly, and sweetly. Make this a happy time, not a frustrating, hurtful time.

Finding a Great Groomer

Most Yorkies go to a groomer regularly, so you should choose that person carefully. Groomers aren't required to have any special training or certification. Most are self-taught. As a result, the abilities and professionalism in the field range widely. Ask for recommendations from your breeder and your veterinarian. Some groomers have worked hard to earn the designation of "Certified Professional Groomer" from International Professional Groomers, Inc. This organization provides training, testing, and information to professional groomers, so membership is a sign of commitment to the profession from the people who participate. The organization's testing program includes written and applied grooming skills; a "Certified Professional Groomer" designation is a standard of excellence in the industry.

Go visit the groomer—see if you like the facility and the groomer's rapport with dogs. Start bringing your puppy in for grooming when he's young, so your pup learns that grooming is a normal part of his life.

When you come to a mat, hold the hair above the mat, and work the mat out with the brush (or your comb). If combing the mat out hurts your dog, just snip it out with your scissors (unless you are planning to show your dog). Your dog's hair will grow back in sooner or later, and no mat is worth causing your dog pain.

After you've thoroughly brushed every inch of your dog, take a metal comb and comb every inch. You'll soon discover that brushes miss a lot of mats—especially the mats that are still small.

Be especially careful when combing your dog's face. Brush out any bits of food that might have accumulated around your Yorkie's mouth. If he has any discharge around his eyes, clean that up with a damp washcloth. Some people use a very fine toothed comb, such as a flea comb, to carefully comb out any discharge that still remains near the eyes after it has been wiped off with a washcloth.

Be very gentle combing around his ears, and be vigilant about thoroughly combing behind them. The fine hair there is a prime place for mats to quickly accumulate. Of course, you also should be very gentle when you're combing and brushing around your dog's genital area.

When you're done, gently touch your dog all over. Do you feel any lumps or bumps? Is he feeling a little thin, or do you have a portly Yorkie? Your regular grooming sessions with your dog are a great time to do a little health check and catch potential problems long before they are crises.

While you're grooming, talk sweetly and happily to your dog. Some people sing. Tell him he's handsome and that you love him

Tying the Knot

It's important to keep your Yorkie's hair out of his eyes, because constant irritation from hair can damage a dog's eyes. You can keep your Yorkie's hair out of his eyes by giving him a short, Westie-style cut around his face. You also can do it by tying the longer hair in your Yorkie's topknot in a rubber band, decorated with a bow. Traditionally, Yorkies always wear one or two red bows.

People who show their Yorkies make an art out of constructing the perfect topknot. At home, you'll probably just want to gather the topknot in your hand, comb it forward, then gently pull it back and tie it with a rubber band. You can put a red bow around the rubber band. Be sure not to pull the hair too tight, though, or it will be uncomfortable for your dog and even could lead to hair loss.

Traditionally, a Yorkie's topknot is decorated with a red bow.

and that he's gorgeous. Make grooming time the highlight of the day—something you both truly enjoy.

Bathing Your Yorkie

Yorkies need more frequent bathing than most breeds. Each dog will vary in his accumulation of oils in the coat, but most Yorkies need to be bathed every week or two. Be calm and gentle. Don't rush, and don't get frustrated. If you get upset, your dog will be more wriggly and difficult.

Always thoroughly brush and comb your Yorkie before you bathe him. If your dog has any mats in his hair when you bathe him, they will become extremely difficult to get out. Start with a dog who is well brushed, bathe him, and then brush him again. That may sound like a lot of work, but it's much less work than trying to get the mats out once they're set in by a bath.

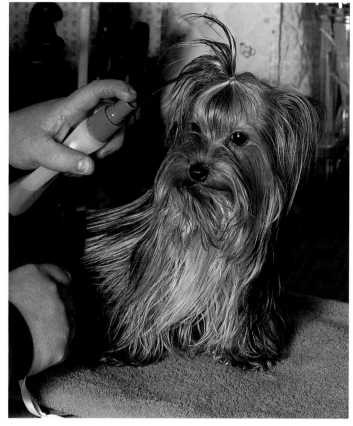

Rather than brushing or combing your dog's dry coat, you should spritz his hair with a conditioning spray first.

Put a nonskid mat in the sink so that the experience isn't scary for your little guy. You can buy an inexpensive rubber bath mat at your local store and just cut it down to size for your sink. Be sure there's a filter across the water drain so that your dog's paws can't slip into the drain, scaring or even hurting him.

Next, be sure that the water temperature feels just slightly warm on your skin. Your little dog has very sensitive skin, and it hurts if the water is too warm. It also isn't any fun if the water is too cold. Your Yorkie is really taking a shower in the sink, not a bath. You should run water over his coat to get it wet, apply shampoo and conditioner, and then rinse. You don't want to keep any water in the bottom of this sink; it all should go down the drain.

Even though a Yorkie's hair is very much like a human's, his

It's a Wrap

Show dogs are judged in large part on their flowing coats. Most show exhibitors wrap their Yorkie's coats when the dog isn't in the ring. Think of it as putting dogs in curlers of sorts. A show Yorkie will have several wraps keeping his hair out of harm's way, including wraps on each side of his muzzle, several along each side of his body, some on his chest, and even one on his tail. Most often, show exhibitors use paper such as rice paper or other acid-free papers, although sometimes they'll use wax paper. They carefully put conditioner on the coat, fold the paper into thirds (like a letter going into an envelope), place the hair in the paper, and fold the paper into a neat little packet.

It may appear a little strange to see a Yorkie trotting along covered with wrapped papers, but wrapping gives a show dog the freedom to run, play, and explore like a dog and still win in the ring.

Most show exhibitors "wrap" their Yorkie's coats when the dog isn't in the ring, a process that keeps the hair from getting broken or tangled.

skin and coat still have the chemical makeup of a dog's. Most "people" shampoos will leave your dog's skin dry, itchy, and flaking. Use a good-quality dog shampoo. Also, use a conditioner formulated for dogs, because it will help keep tangling to a minimum.

Gently massage the shampoo and then the conditioner into his hair. Don't rub or scrub, or else you'll have mats to deal with. When the shampoo and conditioner have been thoroughly massaged on all parts of the dog, rinse thoroughly. Then rinse again. And again. And one more time for good measure. It's very helpful to have a hose attachment of some kind on your sink so that you can direct the spray to thoroughly rinse all those tough-to-reach spots. Nothing can cause more irritation to your dog's skin and make his coat look duller than shampoo that didn't get rinsed out.

Be especially careful when you're washing your little guy's head and face. Many Yorkie owners use a "no tears" shampoo so that they don't have to worry about getting soap in their dog's eyes. When you're finished, rinse very gently around the dog's head. After he's thoroughly rinsed, it's time to dry him. Be sure the place where you dry him has a towel or mat down for solid footing. Start by completely towel-drying your little guy. Be careful while you do this to hold and gently squeeze rather than rub—remember, you don't want to create mats!

Comb out his hair, being sure to get out any tangles at his elbows, behind his ears, and on his tummy—all the places that are

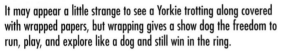

Dewclaws

Don't forget to trim the nails on your Yorkshire Terrier's dewclaws, if he has them. (Dewclaws are the little toes located on your dog's ankles.) These nails grow very quickly, because they don't ever receive any wear. If left untrimmed, they can fairly quickly grow into your dog's skin. Prevention is key, and regularly checking and trimming your dog's dewclaws isn't hard to do.

easy to overlook. If it's a warm summer day, it might be fine to just let your Yorkie air dry the rest of the way. Most of the time, though, you'll also want to blow dry your dog. It's best if you use a dryer specifically designed for dogs. (There's at least one brand that's a portable little dryer that will sit on your counter, leaving your hands free.) You also can find stands to place human hair dryers that will leave your hands free to groom your Yorkie—always a good idea. If you're using a human dryer, be sure to set the temperature on the lowest setting. Your dog's skin is very sensitive, and a hot dryer will hurt. Keep the volume on low as well; the air at full blast will practically blow a little Yorkie off the counter.

Remember, your Yorkie's hair will flow in the direction the dryer is pointed. Gently brush the way you want the coat to go as you dry the hair. All the while, tell your dog he's wonderful and gorgeous, and that time with a dryer is worth it. He'll learn that it's just part of life as a Yorkie.

TRIMMING YOUR YORKIE'S NAILS

Long nails on your Yorkie aren't just an inconvenience—they're also painful. If you can hear his nails clicking when he walks, that means with every step he takes, his nails are pushing against his feet.

When bathing your Yorkie, gently massage the shampoo and then the conditioner into his hair.

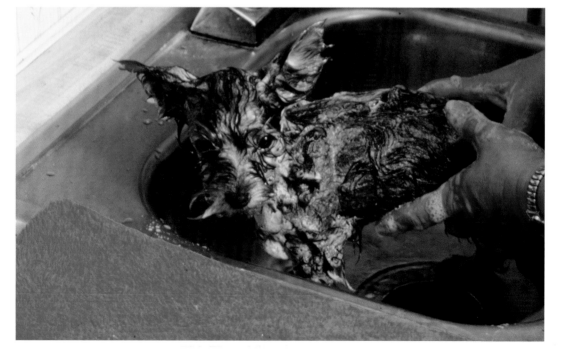

Trimming your Yorkie's nails is a simple and painless part of the grooming process.

Fortunately, most Yorkies have nails that are easy to trim. Position your dog on your lap or put him on a table. Hold your dog's paw in your hand and snip off the very tip of the nail. For most Yorkies, cat nail clippers work wonderfully; they're small, and for most people, they are easier to control than guillotine-style nail clippers. Just trim the very tips of the nails; you don't want to hit the quick (the nerves and blood vessels that run through your dog's nail). If your dog's nails are very long, don't try to get to a short nail all at once. Trim a little bit each week. Over time, the quick inside your dog's nail will retreat, and your Yorkie soon will enjoy the comfortable feeling that comes with well-trimmed nails.

If you work slowly and carefully, there is no reason to ever nick the quick and make your dog bleed. If this does happen, just hold the end of your Yorkie's nail against the tip of your finger, and the bleeding will quickly stop.

If your dog pulls his feet away when you try to trim his toenails, get him accustomed to you touching his feet without the nail clipper. Just hold his paw gently, and if he pulls away, move your hand with it so you're never pulling at his foot. Eventually, he'll give up and let you just hold his foot. Tell him he's a good dog, give him a treat, and repeat the exercise every day. Over time, begin to rub his paw gently and massage between his toes. Once he's comfortable having his feet held and rubbed, he won't be upset when you trim his toenails.

If you have a very wriggly puppy (a distinct possibility with a Yorkie!) or if the concept of cutting your dog's nails just seems too much for you, don't hesitate to make extra visits to the groomer for nail trims. (Nail trims are inexpensive.) While you're at the groomer, you can ask her to show you how to trim your dog's nails yourself.

EAR CARE

Check your Yorkie's ears every time you brush him. Do they smell clean and fresh? Is there any accumulation of wax? If you see some wax, clean out your dog's ears with a ball of cotton. Don't stick a cotton swab into his ears; a quick movement of your Yorkie's head could seriously harm your dog.

If your Yorkie has an excessive amount of ear wax or an unpleasant odor in his ears, make an appointment with his veterinarian. It could be a sign of something that needs medical attention, such as an ear infection or ear mites. It also could be an indication of allergies, or your Yorkie could need a deep ear cleaning, which should be performed by a professional.

Yorkies have hair that grows in their ears that may need to be plucked. Ask your groomer or veterinarian to show you how to pluck these hairs as painlessly as possible.

EYE CARE

Stray hairs in your dog's eyes can hurt him just as much as hair in your eyes hurts you. Keep your dog's hair pulled back in a topknot or trimmed so he doesn't have to deal with hair. Also, watch carefully for signs that your dog's eyes are paining him, such as pawing at or squinting them. If you think your dog's eyes

Trimming Hairy Toes

A Yorkie's hair grows quite long quite rapidly between his toes, especially if your dog doesn't walk on sidewalks or other rough surfaces a lot. When you trim your dog's nails, check out his feet. Using a pair of blunt-nosed scissors, snip away excess hair from the bottom of the foot. You also can tidy up the sides of the feet.

Your Yorkie's Delicate Bones

Yorkshire Terriers, especially puppies, have delicate bones. If your Yorkie takes a flying leap from the counter, he could break his leg or do even worse damage. If he's wriggly, you might want to start out washing him in the bathtub. Of course, you must never, ever leave your Yorkie unattended for a single second on a counter top or other tall place. If you realize you forgot to put your brush on the counter, pick up your wet dog and carry him with you while you look for the brush. You never would forgive yourself if your Yorkie got hurt because you turned your eyes away.

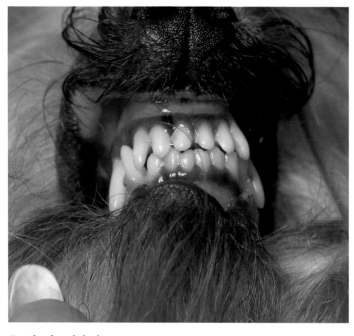

Regular dental checks are a good idea because they will alert you to any changes in your Yorkie's oral health.

might have been injured, take him to your veterinarian immediately.

You can help your dog avoid eye problems by keeping his face clean. Gently wipe around his eyes with a damp, soft cloth or cotton ball when you comb him. Some dogs tend to accumulate "gunk" around their eyes—mucus that flows from the eyes onto the face, so you should soften the accumulation with water and gently rub. You also can comb around the eyes with a fine-toothed comb, but remember to be very gentle. A significant accumulation of matter around the eye could be a sign of an eye injury, so be sure to discuss this with your veterinarian if you have any questions or concerns.

Take regular, gentle care of your Yorkie's eyes. Nothing shows the character of this breed better than its bright-eyed, happy look—and nothing is sadder than a dog whose eyes are in pain.

BRUSHING YOUR YORKIE'S TEETH

Little dogs have big dental problems, and Yorkies are no exception. Your Yorkie has a full complement of teeth in his tiny mouth. The sad fact is that he's likely to lose a good number of those teeth during his lifetime. Even worse, the buildup of bacteria in a dog's mouth can lead to kidney, liver, and heart problems. This is why it's important to take excellent care of your Yorkie's teeth.

The best thing you can do is to brush your dog's teeth daily. If you can't manage that often, promise your dog you'll brush at least twice a week. (Think how unpleasant your mouth would feel if you only were getting your teeth brushed twice a week—and it's a lucky dog who gets that level of care.)

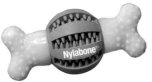

Your veterinarian can supply you with toothpaste formulated just for dogs. It comes in several flavors, although most dogs prefer

a poultry flavor. This type of toothpaste has enzymes that will help break down plaque. Don't use human toothpaste, because it will upset your Yorkie's tummy.

Apply the doggy toothpaste with a gauze pad, a small rubber brush that attaches to your finger, a cat toothbrush, or a child's toothbrush. It can be hard to reach your Yorkie's back teeth, but it's important to do so to keep your dog's mouth free of disease.

To promote dental health, encourage your dog to chew on safe toys such as Nylabones. Many Yorkies love playing with fuzzy toys, too. Throw the toy, play tug-of-war, and encourage him to squeak the squeaker inside. These toys can act much like dental floss, reducing the buildup of plaque. Gummy bones are also safe toys that can help eliminate plaque buildup.

When it's necessary, your veterinarian will recommend that you have your Yorkie's teeth cleaned professionally. (This requires your dog to undergo general anesthesia at the veterinarian's office.) Just like in people, the accumulation of plaque varies widely among individuals. Some Yorkies need teeth cleaning every six months, while others may be able to go a couple of years between cleanings. Remember: The more you brush your dog's teeth and give him chew toys to reduce tartar and plaque buildup, the less he'll need a professional teeth cleaning.

Your Yorkie's beauty is more than just skin deep. Grooming keeps your dog healthy and feeling good, and it helps to solidify the bond between the two of you. What could be more beautiful than that?

Trimming Your Yorkie's Ears

The breed's small, erect ears are part of what makes a Yorkie look so alert. Sometimes, the hair on a puppy's ears actually can train the ears to fall over, which causes them to lose that alert look.

Be sure to keep your puppy's ears trimmed regularly. Generally, the top third of the ear is shaved on the inside and outside. Most adult Yorkies also have the top third of their ears shaved short to keep their attractive appearance as part of their grooming, but it doesn't affect the carriage of their ears as it does when they are puppies.

Hey, Dog Breath!

Your Yorkie's breath shouldn't take your breath away if you come near! Bad breath is a sign that his mouth if full of bacteria—and those bacteria are dangerous to his overall health. Bad breath also can be a symptom of several diseases, including serious kidney and liver problems.

If your dog's breath smells bad, or if you notice a change in the odor of your dog's breath, make an appointment with your veterinarian.

TRAINING AND BEHAVIOR
of the Yorkshire Terrier

f you understand the breed history of the Yorkie, you will understand the challenge of training him. Yorkies are terriers. They were bred to go flying into a dark hole and kill rats. If there were lots of rats, the brave little guy had to keep going after them until they were all gone. Never mind if the rodent was bigger than the dog—he'd stick to it until he finished the job. This work took courage, pluck, and independence. Contrast this with what Border Collies are bred to do. Take the sheep across a river? Okay, if that's what you want. Or compare a Yorkie's background with a Golden Retriever. These dogs were bred to go after birds and return them, unharmed, to their owners.

If you think that you can use the same kind of training that you used for a Border Collie or a Golden Retriever on your Yorkie, you will be in for quite a surprise. Tell a terrier "no" and you won't get cooperation—you'll get defiance. No mere human ever won a war of wills with a Yorkshire Terrier.

There's another side to Yorkies that makes training them even more of a challenge. Yorkies picked up a gentle, soft side during their years as parlor pets. While part of their nature is tough and independent, the other side is soft and can shut down emotionally when he feels overwhelmed. Yelling at a Yorkie or inflicting any kind of violence at all will break the bond of trust that your dog needs from you.

Happily, using today's modern methods, not only can you train your little dog, but he can excel. Yorkies love food, they love fun, and most of all, they love your companionship. Bring them all together, and you and your Yorkie will have a marvelous time together.

This chapter will give you all the tools you need to create a happy, safe, reliable little dog who is well mannered at home and who loves to be with you.

YORKIE SOCIALIZATION

Maybe it's the pull between the independent terrier personality and the devoted companion dog, but Yorkies tend to become either shy or aggressive—or a sometimes unpredictable combination of both—if they aren't properly socialized.

All puppies need socialization to truly enjoy being around people, new places, and other dogs. This is even truer for Yorkies than most other breeds. For the happiness and safety of your little buddy, you must expect to intensively socialize your Yorkie puppy. If you don't, your Yorkie cannot live up to the joyful, exuberant, companionable reputation that the breed earns at its best.

The First Twelve Weeks

At this stage of development, a Yorkie will play with his littermates and learn about limits on behavior from his mother. These experiences will make him a calmer, happier, smarter dog.

Reputable Yorkie breeders don't sell their puppies until they are 12 weeks old, so it's your puppy's breeder who has to take responsibility for the first step of honing her Yorkies' social skills. It is important for the dog to see a variety of people and experience

Puppies must be socialized in order to enjoy being around people and other dogs.

different places during these formative weeks. The love and attention of the breeder is just the beginning, though. You need to kick it up a notch after your dog has settled into your home.

Three Months to Six Months

The first months of your Yorkie's time with you mean socialization, socialization, socialization. After a few days of quiet time when he first comes home with you, take your puppy everywhere you can. Make it your goal to introduce your puppy to 100 kind, friendly, gentle people. Remember, if your puppy meets people or dogs who scare him, he'll learn not to like them. This is why socialization has to be safe, gentle, and sweet.

Expose your little Yorkie to children who are nice. Don't make your puppy endure a child who is grabbing at his fur, running around, or screeching. Look for a quiet, polite child who will listen as you show him or her how to gently pet your dog and give him a little treat.

Give your puppy the chance to experience a variety of objects, such as umbrellas, people on skateboards, power tools, the beach, and cats. Carry tiny treats with you, and give the puppy praise and a tidbit when he explores the world. This teaches him that new experiences are a fun part of the life of a dog.

Watch for signs of stress in your puppy: a tail tucked under the rump, ears down, head down, or yawning. (Yes, yawning in dogs is often a sign of stress!) If you see these signs, back off a distance and slow down. Gradually move closer as your Yorkie accepts the new experience.

Take special care with your Yorkie until his vaccinations are complete. Socialization is extremely important, but so is his protection against such killer diseases as parvo and distemper. Don't let him walk on grass in public parks, rest stops, and other places where unimmunized dogs may have pottied. Carry your Yorkie in your arms if you think it's possible that unimmunized dogs have been in the area. On the other hand, you can go to friends' homes who don't have dogs, or who have dogs who have been well cared for and vaccinated, and let your dog learn to explore on the ground.

When your dog is sturdy enough to walk and play on his own, it's a great idea to sign him up for puppy kindergarten, where he will learn human and dog interaction skills. Be sure the kindergarten doesn't let big puppies pounce on little ones! That just teaches your dog that big dogs aren't to be trusted.

Six Months and Older

Reinforce your good beginning with more classes and experiences. Take an obedience class (positive methods only!). After your dog's bones are fully grown (at about a year old), he can take an agility class. Maybe you'll want to train him for something rewarding, such as animal-assisted therapy.

A surprising number of Yorkie owners just keep their dogs at home, never taking them anywhere. While Yorkies can and do live that way, both you and your dog will miss out on a lot of happy adventures if you never go anywhere together. Trips to the vet and the groomer become increasingly frightening experiences for these unsocialized dogs. The effort to make life seem less scary by staying home has the result of making life more stressful in the long run.

For dogs, learning is a lifelong process, just as it is for humans. Give your Yorkie the gift of letting him, under your safe and loving supervision and guidance, see the wonders that await him in the big, wide world.

CREATING A POSITIVE BOND: CANINE LEADERSHIP 101

Yorkies act like they want to be in charge. They have a terrier-like tendency to run the show. The reality is that your little Yorkie doesn't want to run everything. These dogs need their humans to be their leaders. If we aren't, bossy dogs become unbearable. Shy dogs become petrified. The biggest gift you can give to your dog—and to your relationship with him—is to be a kind, gentle, consistent leader.

If humans don't act like leaders, Yorkies become very stressed and anxious. Imagine how tough life is for a little dog who doesn't think you know how to lead the household. If you aren't acting like a leader from a dog's perspective, he will think you don't know how to take care of him. He will think that he can't count on you. If he goes to the vet's office, he'll feel as if he needs to decide what he'll allow the vet to do, because he won't trust you to make that choice. If a strange person wants to pet him, he will have to decide to allow it, to run, or to fight because he won't think you have the ability to make those decisions for him. When people come to the

Yelling, Hitting, and Losing Your Temper With Your Little Dog

If you find yourself wanting to yell at your Yorkie, or if hitting him seems like a logical idea, take a newspaper, roll it up, and hit yourself over the head. Say, "Stupid human! Stupid, stupid, stupid human!" until you come to your senses. Your dog is the size of a newborn baby. Hitting him, yelling at him, or losing your temper can never, ever get you ahead with your goals.

Enough said!

house, he'll think he needs to decide whether to let them in and figure out where they'll sit.

In short, if you aren't a leader, a bold Yorkie will take over the house. He's likely to become a barker and possibly a growler and nipper. But no matter what these dogs do, they never feel truly safe and secure. They know there's something wrong when the 7-pound (3.2 kg) dog is running the house. It's even worse for shy dogs, who can experience round-the-clock panic if they don't think there's a strong leader in the house to protect them.

You don't have to be violent or even raise your voice to be a leader. You just have to convey

To gain your Yorkie's respect, you must become an authoritative but gentle leader.

leadership in dog terms. Your dog will learn to adore you even more than he did before. He'll also learn to relax. Interestingly, the techniques described below work on all dogs. Brash, pushy, aggressive dogs relax and become nicer, calmer dogs. Shy, fearful dogs relax and become bolder. These little steps are the closest thing to magic that any dog trainer can offer.

Don't Free-Feed Your Yorkie

Give him two meals a day (three or four meals during puppyhood). In doggy terms, the lead dog is in charge of food, so this subtlety tells your dog that you're in charge. This simple bit of advice can do more to change your Yorkie's behavior than any other single thing you can do. It's so simple, yet every single dog on earth will respond to it. For many dogs, it transforms a relationship.

Not only is scheduled feeding a great idea in terms of behavior, but it's good for the health of your little dog. It gives you a chance to monitor his eating habits, which can be the first sign of illness. It also gives you control over his weight. Every dog should be fed meals unless a veterinarian has a specific reason for recommending free-feeding your dog.

Require Your Dog to Sit for His Supper

Asking your dog to sit, down, or perform a trick before eating subtly reinforces that you're in charge of the food. He'll be happy, even proud, to do his little job before being fed.

If your Yorkie is overly pushy, growls at you, or ignores commands that he knows well, you should require him to sit, down, or do a trick before you pet him. Again, this tells him that you're in control of the space.

Grant or Withhold Bed Privileges

Teach him "on" and "off" the bed. When you get in bed, tell him, "Off," and if you want to sleep with him, tell him he can get back on. In a pack situation, the head dog determines who sleeps where.

Make Him Wait at Doorways

Go through doorways in front of your Yorkie. Why? Because the head dog leads the others places and decides who goes where and when. It is a way of silently telling your Yorkie that you are in charge.

HOUSETRAINING YOUR YORKIE

Now that we've covered the basics of canine leadership, we'll continue with housetraining, an issue that creates the most tension between Yorkies and their people. Yorkies, like other toy-sized dogs, are notoriously difficult to housetrain. Difficulty housetraining is the number-one reason why people give up on their Yorkies and turn them over to rescue groups or animal shelters. Even if you never would dream of giving up your pet, having a dog who potties in the house is unpleasant at best and can weaken the bond of love and affection you feel for your pet.

Why Is Housetraining Such a Challenge?

You may have reliably housetrained your Golden Retriever when he was eight weeks old. That's not likely to happen with your Yorkie (or almost any breed of toy dog). If you think about it, it's logical that small dogs are going to have more housetraining

Causes of Housetraining Difficulties

Sometimes housetraining difficulties are caused by a urinary tract infection. Also, some health problems cause a dog to urinate more frequently than normal. If your dog has been previously housetrained and suddenly begins to have housetraining accidents, make an appointment with the veterinarian right away.

If your Yorkie whimpers or cries when he potties, or if he tries to urinate and can't, take him to the veterinarian immediately.

Although Yorkies may be difficult to housetrain, they are perfectly capable of learning to potty outdoors with a little help from you.

trouble than big dogs. Here are some of the reasons:

- They have a different sense of space. Your small dog might eliminate in the corner and feel proud of himself. In his mind, he's gone away as far from his bed as a full-sized dog who's gone to the far end of the yard. Lots of small dogs have trouble grasping the concept of distance.

- They have smaller systems. Yorkie puppies can take a long time for their systems to mature. Your puppy may be six months or older before his system can control urinating or defecating right after meals, exercise, or sleep. Expect to continue to work on the fundamentals of housetraining well into your puppy's adolescence.

- Their genetics may be different. Let's face it: If a Great Dane or Saint Bernard doesn't get the hang of housetraining pretty quickly, he's not likely to stay someone's pet for long. The odds are that dog will never, ever be bred. Because small accidents are so much less difficult to live with, small dogs who have housetraining problems have reproduced for generations. Also, a toy dog may not have the same strong instinct to ask to be let out that a big dog has. (That may be because your living room feels as large as the great outdoors to your little guy.)

- They don't learn to potty outside when they're babies. Recent research by behaviorists has confirmed that dogs develop a preference for where they potty by the time they're eight-and-a-half weeks old. People who breed large dogs usually are making sure their puppies are pottying outside by that age. Toy breeders usually keep their tiny dogs inside during those early weeks so that even with the cleanest, most responsible of breeders, the puppies are pottying on newspaper, bedding, and maybe even carpeting. The lesson is firmly ingrained in your Yorkie before he ever comes home that grass is a weird place to potty.

It all adds up to the fact that you'll have to be more consistent and more patient with a typical Yorkie pup than with a typical Golden Retriever puppy.

What to Do

Don't worry! With a little patience and a lot of consistency and vigilance, your little dog can become reliably housetrained. The following is some advice to help make housetraining easier for both of you.

Make sure to give your dog plenty of opportunities to eliminate outside throughout the day.

Housetraining an Adult Dog

Maybe you've adopted an older Yorkie who isn't reliably housetrained. Maybe you've had your dog since he was a puppy but gave up on the idea that he'd ever learn to potty outside (or in an indoor contained system).

With persistence, your adult Yorkie can be housetrained. You'll both be happier if you work with your dog and help him learn this valuable skill. Train your adult dog by following the same steps as with a puppy. Expect him to take a while to learn the ropes, though, because this is new information for him. With your patient, loving, consistent guidance, your adult Yorkie can learn to be a reliably housetrained dog.

Confine Your Dog

It's not fair to expect your puppy to understand housetraining if you give him free run of the whole house (or the entire living room). He needs to be confined to a space he understands.

Unless he's just pottied, keep him confined to a small area, such as your kitchen or bathroom. When you want him to hang out with you, tie a 6-foot (1.8 m) leash to your waist. He's not likely to potty if he's so close to you, and you'll be able to notice the subtle signs that he needs to potty, because he's right at your feet. (This also teaches him to hang out with you—a great lesson for a companion dog!) When you leave the house, confine your puppy to a crate or an exercise pen.

Take Your Dog Outside

Take your dog outside—don't just put him out there. A small-sized puppy is likely to just be lonely, or he may get distracted. He's not likely to potty on his own. Go out there with him and praise, praise, praise when he potties!

Teach a "Permission to Potty" Command

Teach your puppy a "permission to potty" command. When he potties, say, "Good potty!" (or whatever word you choose) and reward him with pets and maybe even a treat. Eventually, when you say, "Potty!" your dog will potty. This saves enormous amounts of time in your life and is a real help when you're traveling and when you take your dog on unfamiliar surfaces.

Other Tips

Here are a few other tips to keep in mind:
- Never punish your dog for a mistake. It only adds to your small dog's anxiety and slows down the process.

Crates and Punishment

Never, ever use your crate as punishment! If your Yorkie does something naughty and you put him in his crate for a time-out punishment, then you've taught him that he goes into the crate when you're angry. His crate always should be a haven, not a prison.

It's fine to put your dog in a crate with a toy if you need for him to have some quiet time; that's different from putting him in his crate because he was a bad, bad, bad dog!

- Think about your female's comfort. A tall clump of grass that a large dog would never notice is an insurmountable object to a toy-sized female when she tries to urinate. Take her to a part of the yard that doesn't have grass, such as a garden area. You also might have to shovel snow to give her a usable spot.
- Watch for your dog's signs that he needs to go out. Some dogs never get the idea of going to the door and asking to go out. They may come and look at you, or they may circle or trot around restlessly. Learn to read your dog's way of telling you that he needs to potty.
- Have faith. Housetraining your small dog can be a slow process, but one day the light will go on. Your dog can learn this!

Housetraining Problems

Two situations arise in which otherwise well-housetrained dogs urinate in the house: male territorial marking and submissive urination.

Territorial Marking

Male toy dogs are notorious leg lifters. They lift their legs and urinate a small amount to mark territory. This is different from a dog who is pottying, which will be a noticeably larger amount of urine. A male dog can be otherwise perfectly housetrained but still mark. This is particularly a problem in houses with multiple unneutered, male, toy-sized dogs.

Neutering your dog, especially when he's a puppy, is the best defense against territorial leg lifting. Also, rather than keep an eagle eye on their dogs 24 hours a day, many people resort to putting belly bands (also called cummerbunds) on their male dogs. This is a strip of cloth that goes around the dog's tummy, lined with an absorbent pad to manage the problem.

Submissive Urination

Many shy dogs will urinate when you pet them, greet them, or when they're excited. Submissive urination is a dog's way of telling you that he's no challenge to you; the dog is acknowledging in doggy terms that you're in charge.

Don't respond to submissive urination by yelling at the dog! Because these dogs are urinating to show they're submissive to you, they only will urinate more if you yell.

Instead, do the following to build the dog's confidence:

- Greet the dog with your hand under his chin, rather than over his head. The scariest greeting for any dog is for a hand to come over his head or back. The threat of this greeting is multiplied times ten if the dog is tiny.
- Be very matter-of-fact when you come and go. Drama adds to the dog's need to urinate, so if you greet the dog slowly and casually, he will be less likely to turn on the flood.
- Place a washable mat at the front door, so that if your dog does "leak" as he greets you, it's not a big deal. Just wash the mat.
- Do the other exercises in this book to build your dog's confidence. Teach him obedience, and practice the gentle leadership techniques described in this chapter. As your dog gains confidence, his need to submissively urinate will be reduced and probably eliminated.

Indoor Toilet Systems for Small Dogs

Don't leave your Yorkie outside when you're not there to supervise, even if you have a securely fenced yard. It's too easy for your dog to scramble through a mouse-sized fence hole, use his terrier instincts to dig underneath the gate, or hurt himself. That doesn't even begin to describe just how much danger he is in if someone is cruising the neighborhood to steal dogs; an adorable Yorkshire Terrier can bring big bucks among unscrupulous people.

If you can't be home often enough to give your dog a potty break, don't risk letting him run in and out through a doggy door. Instead, bring the outside in and create an indoor toilet system for your dog.

Teach "Permission to Potty" in Your Indoor System

Housetraining pads are treated with an attractive (to a dog) odor, so that your dog will have a clue that it's okay to potty on that spot. To encourage your dog to potty in his litter box or grass box, place a little of his waste on the spot. When you know that he needs to potty, take him over to his box or pad. Give him your permission-to-potty command, "Potty!" If he gets the idea, great. If not, keep taking him to this spot when he needs to eliminate, and keep telling him to potty. When you leave your home, confine the dog in the same room with his box or pads. If he needs to potty in your absence, he's already been introduced to the system, and he's likely to use it when the need arises.

It's okay to take your dog outside sometimes for pottying and let him use his indoor system other times. After all, each is an area where he's had permission to potty.

Housetraining Pads

Pet supply stores have housetraining pads that can be a practical solution for small indoor dogs over the long term. You place the pads on the floor. The pads have been treated with an odor that humans don't smell but that smells like urine to a dog. Most Yorkies will urinate and defecate right on the pad.

Housetraining pads have absorbent material and plastic backing (kind of like a larger, thinner disposable baby diaper), so that you can leave them on most floors without damaging the floors' surface.

Many people who live in condominiums or who must leave their dogs for longer periods of time than is comfortable for the dog find these pads practical and convenient, and they use them during the entire lives of their small dogs.

Litter Boxes

If you have a cat, he probably uses a litter box. If you have a dog who is sort of the size of a cat, he might do great with his own litter box.

Line a large-sized cat litter box (or larger short-sided plastic box of any kind) with an absorbent material. You can buy dog litter. You also can experiment with cat litter, but be sure not to use clumping litter. (If your dog swallows clumping litter, it will form into a solid mass in his tummy, and he might require emergency surgery if it gets caught in his digestive system.)

Be advised that you never should allow your cat and dog to share the same litter box. Your dog is likely to find the cat waste delicious. Worse yet, your cat might resent this intrusion into his most personal space, and he may decide not to use his litter box anymore!

Grass Boxes

If you're a handy person (or know one), you can create a large planter-type box of grass for your dog. This can be ideal for condo dwellers who have balconies. Your mini dog will have a mini lawn of his own!

Even if you're not the Earth Mother type, you can purchase some sod to place in a large box. The sod will live with minimal care quite a while, and you can replace it as needed.

CRATE TRAINING YOUR YORKIE

Nobody thinks it's cruel for a child to have his or her own bedroom, so you shouldn't feel it's cruel for your Yorkie to have his own crate. Dogs get along so well with humans because they both love to live in dens. Humans view their homes as their dens, and your Yorkie will see his crate as a place of his very own where he's safe and secure no matter what else is going on.

Crate Appearance

Your Yorkie's crate should be a comfortable haven. It should be large enough for him to stand in and turn around. However, especially if you're using it as part of a housetraining regimen, you don't want it to be too large. (If the crate is too large, your puppy may be tempted to use a part of it as his personal potty area.) If it will comfortably accommodate a Great Dane, it might not help with housetraining.

Your Yorkie's crate should be comfy. Make sure it has a nice, thick pad for snuggling. (If he tends to chew dog beds, line it with towels.) Your dog

also should have toys in his crate that he can chew. From a dog's perspective, who wouldn't like this nice little spot?

How to Crate Train

It's easy to teach your Yorkie to enjoy his crate. Start out by putting a treat in the crate and letting him eat the treat. Later, close the door briefly once your Yorkie has ventured inside. When you ask your dog to go into his crate, use a consistent command, such as "Crate!" or "Go kennel!" and reward him for going inside. Over the course of a couple of days, gradually work the dog up to staying in the crate for two-hour increments.

Place the crate in an area where your Yorkie feels like he's a part of the family, such as in the living room or the bedroom. You also should feed your dog his meals in the crate to further reinforce the idea of the crate as a happy place.

Build up the time your Yorkie spends in his crate so that he's happy and comfortable there when you leave the house and when he sleeps at night.

How Much Is too Much Crate Time?

Kids don't live in their bedrooms all day long, and dogs shouldn't live in their crates for endless hours at a time. How much crate time is too much depends on your dog and what other things happen to him during the day. If he gets plenty of fun, exercise, and interaction with you before and after being in his crate, then he can comfortably hang out in the confined space for longer than if he's just stuck in there because you're busy. If he's confined to a crate while you're at work, come home at lunch to let him out and play with him so that he can stretch his legs and have some fun.

If your Yorkie has any housetraining accidents in his crate,

Crates in the Car

It's dangerous for your Yorkie to ride loose in the car. An airbag can kill a human child, and it also can kill your little dog. Keep a crate in the rear of the car, strapped in with a seatbelt. Think of it as a child safety seat for your dog. If your Yorkie is accustomed to riding in a crate, he'll happily jump into it as part of the fun of riding in a car. You'll be driving with peace of mind knowing that your Yorkie is safe.

Retractable Leashes

Retractable leashes are very popular. They allow the dog to reel out a line that is as long as 25 feet (7.6 m). Think about the length of that line when you're walking on city streets, however. You know that Yorkies love to hunt. If your dog sees a cat or squirrel, you don't have control for that 25 feet (7.6 m). If a car is coming, your dog can run right in front of it. Yorkies are so fast and so small, the driver would never see your dog until it's too late.

When you're walking on a sidewalk, be sure to keep the length of the leash locked into a distance that keeps your dog safe from traffic. The best thing to do is to forget the retractable leash and simply use a 6-foot (1.8 m) leash , which still allows your dog plenty of room to walk. If you feel you must use a retractable leash, please be careful.

this is a serious sign he has been in the crate too long. Don't let this happen again, or it can be very, very hard to get your dog to accept a crate. This also can slow down the housetraining process enormously!

After your Yorkie is accustomed to wearing his collar or harness, you can begin training him to walk on a leash.

LEASH TRAINING

Your Yorkie has four feet for a reason—he's a dog, and he loves to go for walks! When you first try to take a Yorkie for a walk, it may not seem like that's what you're doing. Your little guy might feel more like a kite than a dog—jumping in every direction, barking at big dogs, and starting and stopping at unpredictable moments. A worried Yorkie might do the opposite. He'll stand and not move, period. However, believe it or not, in a couple of days you and your Yorkie can walk together joyfully. It just takes some practice.

Choosing a Collar and Leash

Never use a choke chain on your Yorkie. One of the breed's biggest health concerns is collapsing tracheas. A choke collar can badly injure your Yorkie if he has that condition. Even if your Yorkie doesn't have any problems with his trachea, there is no reason to ever use a choke collar on a little Yorkie; other collars are way more effective.

Use a regular buckle collar or one that snaps. Also, if your dog pulls against his collar or coughs or hacks when it's around his neck, consider using a harness. The training techniques in this book don't use force, so a harness or a collar will work equally well. Choose whichever works best for you and your Yorkie. With the increasing popularity of tiny dogs, you'll probably be able to find collars or harnesses that fit your little guy at your local pet supply store.

If you have trouble finding dog collars or harnesses, do not substitute a cat collar or harness. These products are designed with "breakaway" features, which means the collar will stretch or unsnap when it's pulled. You could lose your Yorkie if you use a cat collar. Plenty of Internet sites offer products for tiny dogs, so use one of those if you can't find a product that fits your dog at your local store. Dog shows are also a great place to find tiny products.

Most dog trainers recommend a 6-foot-long (1.8 m) leash for training. It's short enough for controlling your dog but long enough to train commands like stay and come.

Introducing Your Yorkie Puppy to a Collar and Leash

Gradually introduce your Yorkie to his collar, and be sure that the collar you have chosen is not too tight or too loose. You should be able to put one finger inside the collar. If it's too tight, it's obviously uncomfortable for your little guy. If it's too loose, he can get it caught on something or slip out of it. A young Yorkie is an amazingly inventive creature, and he quickly can end up with a collar stuck in his mouth, a paw hopelessly tangled in the collar, and goodness knows what else. Especially during those first days, watch him carefully when he has his collar on.

Your Yorkie may scratch and shake his head—after all, the puppy has never had anything around his little neck before. Just tell him how handsome he is in his fabulous new collar, and give him a treat and play with him. As long as the collar is properly fitted, it won't take long for him to get used to having something around his neck.

If you decide to use a harness rather than a collar, follow the same procedure as described for becoming accustomed to the

Don't Be a "Jerk!"

In the bad old days, we used to teach dogs to walk with us by jerking on the leash. This is a bad idea for any dog, and it's a terrible idea for your Yorkie, who has a delicate neck. Rather than jerking on the leash, when you change directions, warn your dog by saying, "Let's go!" and showing him a treat or patting your lower leg. This exercise should teach your dog that it's fun to follow you, not that it's painful!

collar. In either case, your Yorkie quickly should become accustomed to wearing something on his body.

The First Leash Experience

After your puppy is completely relaxed and happy wearing his collar or harness, you can start training him to walk on a leash. For the first day or two, let him lead you. Put his lightweight leash on (remember, your puppy is a little dog and doesn't need a leash that can restrain a Rottweiler), and let him lead the way. Tell him he's wonderful, give him treats, and just follow him. If he wants to just stand still, that's okay, too. Give him a treat, and tell him he's great.

As soon as your dog is relaxed and comfortable leading you, it's time for you to lead him. Show him a treat, and have him take a few steps with you. Then let him lead you. Then show him a treat and have him come with you. Soon, he'll love seeing his leash and will enjoy walking new places with you.

Teaching your dog basic obedience will help him become a well-behaved canine companion.

Teaching Your Yorkie to Walk on a Leash

Think about what walks with your dog are like. Is he pulling on the lead, maybe even choking himself in his efforts to go farther, faster? Or is he worried, even shaking, when you go places, hiding behind your ankles? Does he suddenly stop, and you worry about tripping over your dog?

In any case, walking with a dog who doesn't cooperate isn't very much fun for you, and it's not a lot of fun for the dog, either. Teaching your Yorkie to walk calmly on a loose leash will be a gift for both of you. Fortunately, teaching your dog to walk calmly on a loose leash usually doesn't take very long.

"Let's Go!"

To begin, your dog should be wearing a comfortable buckle or snap collar, and you should have a lightweight 4-foot (1.2 m) or 6-foot (1.8 m) leash (not a flexible or retractable leash). At first, practice someplace with low distractions, such as your living room or backyard.

Say, "Let's go" (or "walkies" or whatever word or phrase suits you) and start walking. If your dog pulls, turn in the other direction and say, "Let's go!" the instant his leash tightens. If he runs out and pulls in the new direction, turn and go a different way, saying, "Let's go!"

The moment he's walking on a loose leash, give him an easily chewed treat and tell him he's an extremely good dog. Very quickly, your dog will figure out that he never, ever will get where he wants to go if he pulls. On the other hand, keeping an eye on you is incredibly fun. Soon, he will be merrily walking on a loose leash.

Start out practicing in your living room or backyard, where there aren't any distractions. Once you've really mastered *let's go* in a place with low distractions, practice it somewhere with more noises, smells, and activities. Even if you feel silly, continue practicing the leash walking procedures described earlier. If you consistently, adamantly follow them, your dog will be walking nicely with you within a week.

Some dog trainers give a variation of the technique I've described. They suggest that you merely stop when the dog comes to the end of the leash and wait for him to calm down before going

Looking at Food Through a Dog's Eyes

When you first teach your dog *watch me*, he isn't really watching you. He's watching the yummy treat that you're holding between your eyes. It's easy to dismiss the importance of what you're teaching your dog with this technique.

All dogs need leadership, and small dogs (and remember, they really do know they're small) crave it most of all. In doggy terms, the creature who has control of the food is the leader. So, at first, your dog is looking in your eyes and thinking, "I just want the treat! NOW!" But soon the treat will disappear from your face, and he'll still be staring lovingly at the spot where you once held it. He will transfer his feelings about the treat to you as a leader.

Humans do much the same thing when they feel warm and personally close to people who are rich, powerful, or famous. That treat in your face translates to you seeming powerful and rich, in doggy terms.

forward. You can always try this method since it will make you a bit less dizzy than changing directions, but it probably won't work with your Yorkie. Why? Because Yorkies can amuse themselves mightily on just a leash length. They will circle, jump, and bark. If you have a busy little dog—and that's usually the kind of dog who's at the end of a leash—mostly you will need to change directions for him to realize that being in charge isn't as much fun as being a follower!

Of course, you might feel a bit dizzy changing directions several times. And you might be worried about what the neighbors will say (although this certainly can't be the oddest thing they've seen you do!). But if you follow this technique for just a few days, you'll have a lifetime of happy, calm, connective walks together.

Keeping His Eye on You

Teaching your dog *watch me* is the first step toward teaching a number of other commands. If you can keep his focus on you instead of any nearby distractions, he will be much more likely to learn what you are trying to teach him.

PRE-OBEDIENCE LESSONS

The *watch me* and *catch* commands make all other obedience lessons infinitely easier to teach. A dog who is looking at you is more likely to learn what you teach him, just as kids in school are more likely to learn when they watch their teacher.

Watch Me

Watch me may be the most important lesson you teach your dog. If your Yorkie is looking you in the eye, he can't issue a challenge to a big dog. It's physically impossible. It takes eye contact for your dog to chase a car, bark at a cat, or become aggressive with a big dog. However, if your dog is staring at your eyes, he can't create any trouble for himself.

Watch me is extremely practical. The next time your Yorkie wants to yap at that nasty dog down the street, you can say, "Watch me." Your dog will focus on you, and the problem will be resolved. This simple command does something more profound, as well. Once you teach your dog *watch me*, your relationship with your dog may dramatically improve in a matter of days. He'll be looking to you for leadership and fun. You'll be becoming someone he wants to follow around, and that's the first step in strengthening the bond between the two of you.

Teaching Watch Me

Hold a treat between your eyes and say, "Watch me." Your Yorkie will stare at you longingly. Well, he'll stare at the treat, but

Positive training methods reward your dog for a job well done with a treat, praise, or a favorite toy.

since the treat is between your eyes, he'll be focusing in your direction. Instantly say, "Good watch me!" (or click your clicker) and reward the dog with the treat.

After the dog is looking at you consistently, hold the treat in your hand (out of sight of the dog). Say, "Watch me." If he looks at you, say, "Good watch me!" (or click your clicker) and reward him. If he looks at your hand, say, "Uh-uh, watch me." If he looks at your face, reward him. If he doesn't understand, then hold the treat in front of your eyes again, and remind him of what you want. Practice *watch me* several times a day, always with a food reward.

Over time, mix up holding treats in front of your eyes and having a treat in your hand until you eventually always have the treat in your hand. You also should gradually require your Yorkie to look at you for longer periods of time before giving the reward.

Catch

Once your Yorkie has mastered *watch me*, it's fun to teach him *catch*. Playing catch also rewards your dog for paying attention to you.

Teaching Catch

To teach *catch*, hold a treat just an inch (2.5 cm) over your dog's head and say, "Catch!" Then let go of the treat. If the treat drops to the ground, quickly pick it up and try again. The only time your dog should get the treat is when he catches it in midair. Do this several times, and most dogs will be catching midair in a matter of minutes. Over time, drop the treat from higher and higher distances. This game teaches them to pay attention to you—and that's a good thing!

Some dogs never get the hang of *catch*, because it takes a certain amount of depth perception and eye-mouth coordination that some dogs just don't have. Others never seem to get past the fact that something (even a treat!) is falling out of the sky toward their heads. Every dog can learn *watch me*, but *catch* is just a bonus command that's fun for the majority of dogs.

BASIC COMMANDS—THEY'RE MORE FUN THAN YOU THINK!

Training your Yorkie is a little bit like driving a sports car. These dogs are easy to maneuver, and they're tons of fun. Not only is training fun, but it's important as well. Little Yorkies can get in big trouble. They're fast and independent, and they have a high prey drive. If they don't come when they're called or know that it's important to sit and stay when you ask, your dog can end up dashing through a door, get hit by a car, or be injured by a big dog.

Using positive methods is good with all dog breeds, but it's the only way to train a Yorkie.

To teach sit, hold a treat in front of your Yorkie's nose, and slowly pull the treat over the dog's head.

He needs to learn in a way that makes him feel safe and that can't hurt his little body. Fortunately, that's easy to do.

Modern, positive dog training rewards dogs for good behavior. Some people are resistant to giving their dog a cookie for doing something right. The reality is that studies have proved that dogs learn fastest when they have a reward. This shouldn't be too surprising, because people are the same way. We expect to be paid for our work—and money is a hugely motivating reward for us humans. Money isn't the only reward that matters to us, though. We work harder when someone we respect praises us. In the same vein, treats, lavish praise, petting in a favorite spot, and a special toy are all motivating factors for your Yorkie. With their independent streak, Yorkshire Terriers resist being forced to do things at all costs. Turn it into fun, and they'll surprise you with their quick intelligence and love of learning.

You can use two types of positive training techniques: clicker training and lure-and-reward training. Clicker training uses a clicker, a little hand-held, low-tech device with a metal strip that makes a sharp, distinctive click when you push it. Dogs learn to recognize that the click is a magically good thing by pairing the click with a food reward. Click, treat. Click, treat. Within minutes, every dog loves to hear the click.

After the dog understands that a click means good things, the clicker is used to highlight good behavior. The instant that the dog does something that you like, you click the behavior. Think of a camera click; that clicking sound captures a moment in time. Clicker training captures a dog doing something right and rewards it with a click, and then a treat.

Lure-and-reward training is equally positive. In this method, a lure (such as a yummy treat) helps the dog find the position that you want. For example, if you want your dog to sit, you move the treat over his head, and he follows the treat with his nose until he automatically sits. You've lured him into place with the treat, and you'll reward him with it when he does what you want him to do.

This chapter uses a lure-and-reward system of training, but don't worry. If you like clicker training, just "click" when the instructions tell you to say, "Good!"

Your Ultimate Goal

Advanced obedience dogs do out-of-sight stay exercises when they enter dog shows. All the dogs entered in the class line up together, so a little Yorkie might be next to a Saint Bernard or a Great Dane. The judge orders the handlers to leave their dogs, and the handlers leave the building. The dogs then perform a three-minute sit-stay. The handlers return to their dogs, then put the dogs on a five-minute down-stay and leave the building again. They're doing this exercise in the middle of a dog show where there might be 2,000 other dogs, loudspeakers blaring, and kids eating hot dogs next to the obedience rings.

You may never want to enter a dog show, but think about training your dog to have just as reliable a sit-stay as the dogs who compete at trials. It will provide great peace of mind to know that your dog likely will stay still no matter what, especially when there's an emergency. Remember, though, that five-minute out-of-sight stay exercise started with a simple one-second stay. It's the way dogs learn.

Sit

Before you teach the *sit*, look back to the section of this chapter that explains *watch me*. It will make your task infinitely easier if you have a dog who loves to look adoringly into your eyes.

Teaching Sit

To teach *sit*, you first should hold a treat in front of your Yorkie's nose. Slowly pull the treat over the dog's head, between his ears. Almost all dogs naturally will "rock" back into a sit. Say, "Good sit!" and give the reward while the dog is in the sitting position.

If your Yorkie doesn't automatically sit, gently tuck your finger under his rear to help him go into a sit position.

If your dog is turning around instead of sitting, you might want to practice in a confined space. Put him on a comfortable chair where he feels safe. He'll back up to the back of the chair, and then you can lure him into a sit.

If you notice that your dog is doing a "sit up and beg" position, this means you're holding the treat too high. Hold it just above his nose.

There's a reason why almost every dog trainer starts with the *sit* command—dogs learn it incredibly quickly and easily. Within a matter of a few minutes, almost every dog—young or old, rescue or carefully bred show dog—will be sitting on command. Because it's so common, it's easy to miss the pure magic of this moment. Your dog has just understood what you asked him to do, and he did it. It is from this first moment of true communication that so much more will grow.

Repeat this command no more than three times in a row, but you can practice several times a day.

Important: Don't ever push down on your Yorkie's rear end to make him sit. It can damage any dog and easily can permanently injure a small-breed puppy's hips and back. Also, don't ever pinch his kidneys (as some trainers may show you), as this potentially can harm him internally. Instead, let the treat do the work. Your dog will figure it out. Just be patient, and let him take his time.

Stay

Before you even think about practicing *stay* with your dog, there's an important concept to memorize: Always give your Yorkie the reward when he's doing what you ask him to do.

Keeping It Fun

Don't ever call your Yorkie to you for punishment or something even mildly unpleasant. If you need to clip your dog's nails, for example, go collect him— don't call him. You want this command to represent only the good things. When your little dog sees a cat across the street and a car is coming, you want your dog to think it's better to come to you than to tear across the street after that cat. That won't happen if he thinks you're calling him to trim his nails.

Most people teach their dogs the "un-stay." They say, "Stay! Stay there, boy. Good stay!" The good little dog keeps his butt on the ground and doesn't move a muscle. Finally, the time is up. The little dog succeeded in his *stay*! What does the trainer do? She releases the dog—and then rewards him. So what does the dog learn? That he gets rewarded when he gets up!

When your dog is doing a *sit-stay* (or any other command), reward him while he's doing what you want. The dog will understand much more quickly what you want him to do, and he quickly will become patient, waiting for the reward he knows will be coming to him if he stays still. If you reward a dog consistently while he stays still, then he'll learn to love to do a *sit-stay*.

Teaching Stay

Be sure your dog knows and understands the *sit* command before you start. Although *sit* and *stay* are two different commands, your dog will need to know how to sit before you can proceed to the stay command.

After you tell your dog to sit, take a step back about 6 inches (15.2 cm) and gently say, "Stay, good sit-stay." Instantly and while he is still sitting, reward him. He can't learn to sit for one minute

Teaching your dog to stay on command may save his life in a dangerous situation.

until he's learned to sit for one second. When he succeeds at a one-second *sit-stay*, expand the time to five seconds, then ten seconds, etc. If he consistently gets up after 15 seconds, for example, give him a 12-second stay and reward him. Chain together two or more stays. Tell him to stay and reward after 10 seconds, then step back and tell him, "Stay" and reward him after another 15 seconds. Repeat this command no more than three times in a row, but feel free to practice several times each day.

Sadly, many people teach *stay* as if it is a horrendous punishment. As always, think about what this does to your dog. It's hard enough for a small dog to have the courage to sit and stay while you walk away; this exercise really teaches him to have trust and faith in you. Imagine how much harder it is for this little guy if you're screaming, "STAY! STAY! STAAAAAAYYY!!!"

Just relax and tell him how clever he is for staying, and you and the dog will do better. *Stay* should be every bit as interesting and enjoyable for your Yorkie as shaking hands, rolling over, or jumping for a treat.

Using Words Consistently

If you use the word "down" to mean "off," use another word or phrase for the down command. For example, say, "Lie down" or "Drop." You can't have "down" mean get back on all four feet and also mean lie down on the floor.

Come

The *come* command should be the most joyful, glorious, happy word your Yorkie can hear. He needs to know that when he turns and runs to you, great and wonderful things will happen, like treats, play, kisses, and toys.

Teaching Come

The *come* command must be taught in an enclosed room or a completely fenced-in area. Put your dog on a long leash, but only use it to corral him if he decides to go running in circles. Don't pull on the leash when you teach him this fun, energetic, and lively command.

It seems counterintuitive, but the best way to attract your dog to come to you is to position yourself far across the room. If you're close by, you're old hat. When you're across the room, your dog will be a bit more anxious to come to you. Remember, this must be done in a safe, enclosed room or yard. Don't take chances with your dog's life by hoping he'll learn to come in an open yard.

For the first few weeks, teaching *come* is a two-person job. Someone else must hold the dog while you walk away and call the dog. (If you're both in the same household, it's great to call the dog

If your Yorkie is confused about learning to down on the ground, you can teach him this command on a chair.

back and forth.) The person holding the dog should be silent. You should get the dog revved up and eager to come to you. In a high, happy voice, say, "Ready? Ready? Ready?" Then, call him with a very clear, "Come!"

Be very, very fun when you call your Yorkie. Use a happy voice. Squat down and clap your hands, or turn and run in the other direction. Make yourself interesting and appealing. When your dog comes to you, treat him and praise him for at least 15 seconds. When you come home, your dog doesn't just come up at say, "Good" in a monotone. No way! He bounces up and down and says he's thrilled, just thrilled to see you. He wiggles, he licks, he snuggles! You need to show the same happiness when your dog comes to you on the come command. Your dog needs to know that you're excited he came to you—so act like it!

Practice this command three times a day. Don't overdo this one, because you want to keep it a spontaneous, joyful communication between you and your dog.

What to Do if Your Dog Doesn't Come

Most Yorkies respond to this happy calling with glee and run joyfully to their person. The *come* command is a ton of fun! Occasionally, though, a dog will have a mind of his own. He will meander off or sniff the floor or run around the room madly, despite your best efforts to get him to come to you.

A solution exists that works almost every time, even for the most independent little Yorkie. Without getting upset, gather the dog's long leash and bring him right to you.

Take a treat out of your pocket. (It's important to practice this command with a treat you find edible, such as string cheese or some meat.) Show the dog the treat he could have earned, and say, "Well, I get the treat." Next, pop it in your mouth. Eat the treat like it's the best, most incredible morsel you've ever had in your life. Slurp noisily. Smack your lips. Say just how delicious it is. Don't even think about fake eating the treat. The key is to eat it in front of the dog and swallow it. Your dog will get the message loud and clear: He just lost out on the most incredible reward of his lifetime because he didn't come.

Then, give the dog back to your friend to hold, and show the dog the treat. Once again call him enthusiastically—chances are he'll come running. If he's the rare dog who doesn't, just repeat the process. With him sitting at your feet, eat the treat with enormous gusto.

When teaching stay, reward your dog while he's in the stay, not afterward, or he may think you're rewarding him for the release from the stay.

Give him back to your friend and call him a third time. I've never met a dog who didn't come the third time. When he comes, give him a big "jackpot" treat. Tell him he's great! Make it incredibly worthwhile for him to come to you. Soon, you'll have a dog who has learned that coming is a very rewarding activity.

Separating Stay From Come

It's tempting to teach the *stay* and *come* commands together. After all, that's what you see trained dogs do all the time. The handler says, "Stay," walks across the room, and then calls the dog. What could be more sensible?

If you combine the *stay* and *come* commands too soon, though, your dog will have trouble doing a reliable stay for weeks. He'll soon decide that *stay* means "sit for a few

Finding a Good Trainer

Ask for references for a trainer from your veterinarian and groomer; both are likely to know who does a good job. If a group is doing animal-assisted therapy in your community, they may have recommendations as well. Also, check out trainers through the Association of Pet Dog Trainers, a national organization that provides ongoing education and certification for dog trainers. This organization emphasizes gentle, nonviolent training methods. Their website can be found at www.apdt.com.

seconds and then come running."

A reliable *stay* is a huge safety precaution for your Yorkie. Don't jeopardize it by combining the stay with the come command too early. In my class, I don't let students combine the commands until the dog has clearly understood and practiced both commands separately for at least three weeks.

Down

If you need to keep your Yorkie absolutely still and under control, nothing is more effective than the *down* command. If your dog is committed to a *down-stay*, he's not likely to get up. This is the most stable position in the dog training universe, but it is also the most difficult exercise for a small dog to learn. Think about it a little, and it makes a lot of sense. Small dogs already feel vulnerable. They may be mighty carnivores in their minds, but their bodies look more like rabbits. Putting themselves in a down position, especially near other dogs, makes them feel extremely vulnerable.

The only way a Yorkie can perform this exercise successfully is to completely trust you and to feel safe. That's why your patience and gentleness is especially important with this lesson.

Teaching Down

When teaching the *down*, your dog should be standing and relaxed. (Most books and trainers will tell you to teach *down* from a *sit*. However, dogs who have recently learned to sit and stay are terribly confused when suddenly you tell them to down. If you start from a standing position, they're much less worried when learning this exercise.)

Next, hold a treat between your Yorkie's front toes. He'll reach down for the treat and may drop into a down position. Say, "Good down!" and give him the treat. If he doesn't drop, keep the treat on the floor, pushing it slightly toward his chest. If he physically follows the treat with his nose, his chest will go down on the ground. Say, "Good down," and reward him when his chest rests on the ground.

Be patient. Sometimes it takes some maneuvering before your dog learns to down. If he's getting frustrated, reward his partial success. In other words, if his chest is on the ground but his rear end is still high in the air, give him a treat with a "yes!" for the partial success. Build on the partial success until he downs with his whole body, at which time you should say, "Good down" and treat him generously. As always, repeat a command no more than three times in a row, but you can practice several times a day.

Teaching Down on a Chair

If you had a big dog, you could be assured that your dog would learn the *down* if you held a cookie by his toes. While about 90 percent of small dogs also will learn the *down* using this technique, the other 10 percent won't. Why? Because their noses are already at ground level! If your Yorkie is confused about learning to down on the ground, or if you'd rather not crawl on the floor to teach this, teach your Yorkie the down command on a chair.

The technique for teaching the *down* on a chair or couch is exactly the same as the traditional technique outlined earlier, except you hold the treat a few inches (cm) below the level of the seat. Your Yorkie has to bend his front legs to get to the treat, which means he's well on his way to learning the down. A word of advice: Be sure to set the dog up near the edge of the seat, or he won't be able to follow the treat with his nose over the end of the chair.

Be sure your dog is comfortable and understands the *down* command well on a chair before you try it on the ground. When he really understands it, you should be able to just say, "Down on the ground," and he'll lie down.

The Down-Stay

Once your dog is comfortable doing a *down*, it's time to add the *stay* command to the equation. Teach this lesson exactly the way you taught the *sit-stay*.

After you tell your Yorkie to down, take a step back about 6 inches (15.2 cm) and gently say, "Stay, good down-stay." Instantly and while he is still in the down position, reward him. Just like

Strengthening the Yorkie/Family Bond

It helps your Yorkie to perform better if everyone in the household gives him the same rules and the same commands. It also will help your Yorkie bond to everyone, rather than just a single family member.

with the *sit*, your Yorkie can't learn to down for one minute unless he's learned to down for one second.

When he succeeds at a one-second *down-stay*, expand the time to 5 seconds, then 10 seconds, etc. If he consistently gets up after 15 seconds, for example, give him a 12-second stay and reward him. Help him to succeed.

Chain together two or more stays. Tell him, "Stay" and reward after 10 seconds, and then step back and tell him, "Stay" and reward him after another 15 seconds.

Release

One of the hardest things is for a dog to know when a command is over. He's sitting by your side and watching you, watching you, watching you. You're talking with friends, enjoying yourself. At some point, your dog has to guess when the exercise is over. If he stops doing his task, and you don't say anything, apparently he guessed right. If you get irked or put him back in place when he moves, apparently he guessed wrong. This isn't fair to your little dog.

If your Yorkie won't let people near you when he is in your arms, simply put him on the ground.

Instead of making your dog guess when the lesson is over, teach him a release word. When you say this word, your dog's exercise is finished. He can relax and do whatever he wants to do—or whatever you ask next.

Selecting a Release Word

The most common release word is "okay!" However, this word is used all the time. Because we use "okay" so often without realizing it in casual conversation, you might want to come up with another release word so that your dog doesn't become confused.

Any word or short phrase will do: "At ease!", "You're

The Importance of Consistency

If your dog is going to change his behavior, it is essential that you are absolutely consistent with *your* behavior. You can't allow him to misbehave one day, and even laugh at his behavior, and then tell him his behavior is unacceptable the next. Your dog simply will learn to ignore you and view you as an unreliable person.

Remember, dogs who are growling and snapping aren't happy. Your leadership in helping your dog change will improve the quality of his life, as well as the bond that the two of you share.

done!", "Off duty!", "Free dog!"—any word that sticks well in your mind. The really hip people who herd with their Border Collies say, "That'll do" to release their dogs. You always can use that for your Yorkie, too!

Don't use "good!" or other words of praise as your release word. You want to tell your dog he's good in the middle of an exercise and still have him continue to stay, come, or sit. The release word must be separate and distinct in sound from "good!"

Be sure to give your dog his release word at the end of every exercise, so that he knows when it's done. It will make life easier for him, and it also will make him better able to follow the directions that you give him. He won't be standing up from his sit periodically just to see if the exercise is over. Clarity will help him do a better job.

FINDING A SAFE OBEDIENCE CLASS

It can be fun and worthwhile to take a class with your Yorkshire Terrier. Dog training is a visual, 3-D activity, and especially if you want to do more advanced work with your dog, it helps to work with a capable trainer.

Before considering taking a class or private lessons, check out the trainer. Here are some things to do:

- Talk with the trainer about her philosophy. Does she use modern, motivational methods? Does she believe in food rewards? If so, then she might be a good trainer for a Yorkie. On the other hand, if she's an old-fashioned, jerk-and-pull trainer, you and your dog aren't going to have a lot of fun.
- Ask the trainer what experience she's had training small dogs. Ideally, she's actually had a small dog of her own. Second best is someone who has worked with a lot of small dogs and can give you references from other small dog clients who have succeeded in her classes.

Eliminating Toys

If there's just one thing that makes your dog extremely possessive, consider eliminating it from his routine. In other words, if the only thing that he growls over is a certain toy, get rid of the toy or only allow him to play with it at certain times.

• Observe the trainer's classes for yourself. Are the dogs and people having fun? If you have multiple people in your home, does she welcome family members to participate? Is the class under control, or is it chaos? Most important, do you think it's a place that's safe for your Yorkie? An instructor or class that might be perfectly fine for your neighbor's rowdy Labrador might be a disaster for your little Yorkshire Terrier.

Often, a group class full of big, untrained dogs just isn't a safe place for your little Yorkie. If you find an instructor whom you like, but you aren't comfortable with the beginner's class, talk with the instructor about some alternatives.

One alternative is to ask her to consider teaching a small-dogs only class. She might like the idea. A small-dog class is a trainer's slice of heaven. She won't be worried that any of these dogs is going to bite her arm off—a definite plus from a trainer's perspective! Also, the dogs are fun, and the people who have these dogs are very attached and loving with them, factors that make training them an enjoyable experience for the instructor. Plus, if no one else in the community is teaching a small-dog class, it can be a nice marketing niche for the trainer.

You also can use this book (and any other training books you like) to train your Yorkie well enough so that the trainer will admit you into one of her more advanced classes. If the big dogs are well trained, you won't have to be as worried.

A third alternative is to take private lessons. You'll have the trainer's expertise, but you won't have to worry so much about other dogs. If you do this, though, be sure that you practice in a variety of places, so that your dog is exposed to different sights, sounds, smells, and people.

YORKIE PROBLEM BEHAVIORS

There is a popular comic strip, "Grand Avenue," that has a recurring story line about two evil Yorkies. Left to their own devices, Yorkies can be very barky and aggressive toward strangers (and your friends), as well as toward other dogs. It's easy to understand why someone who doesn't love your dog as much as you do might think he's evil.

Before you dismiss your Yorkie's problem behaviors as stemming from the fact that he "thinks he's a big dog," think again. Yorkies aren't stupid dogs—in fact, they're very smart. Your little

Yorkie knows he's not a big dog. He's behaving aggressively, in all likelihood, because he figures a good offense is the best defense. He's worried.

If you provide leadership and follow the suggestions outlined below, you will have a Yorkie whom everyone else loves. More important, you will have a calm, happy, enthusiastic dog who has the freedom to enjoy being a dog and who doesn't have to spend his time worrying about his territory.

Barking

People who aren't overly fond of Yorkies often call them "yap dogs." They sometimes have a point. Many Yorkies, to put it kindly, are "verbally gifted." In fact, most small-breed dogs bark noticeably more than their larger counterparts. Their constant barking can grate on your nerves like the sound of fingernails on a chalkboard. Small dogs tend to be barkers for several reasons:

- Humans are more forgiving of barking in a small dog. Often, people don't even seem to notice that their dogs are barking; they just talk louder to be heard over the din. If they owned a full-sized dog, though, the same person probably wouldn't put up with the noise.
- Small dogs are more worried than big dogs. When a little dog is barking nonstop, people often will say with a note of pride, "He sure thinks he's a big dog." Nothing could be further from the truth. Nonstop barking is often a sign that the dog is insecure, and he figures that the best defense is a good offense. As a result, he's trying to sound big, brave, and tough in order to feel safe.
- Small dogs are bored. All dogs need physical and mental stimulation. Too often, small dogs are treated more like stuffed

Yorkie Body Language

Often, people believe that their dog bit or lunged or growled with "absolutely no warning." Chances are, he was giving you plenty of warning through his body language, but you just weren't watching.

Aggression is always preceded by a dog becoming tense all over his body. He usually will be absolutely still for a moment before he attacks something. Watch for the tension, and redirect your Yorkie's attention away from whatever he's looking at. If your Yorkie is pulling away and his ears are pulled back while he's growling, he's a scared dog. Take him away from a situation that gives him that much stress (which may be as simple as just picking him up and turning his face in a different direction).

Sometimes people misread a Yorkie's intention. While certain Yorkies can growl and bare their teeth, many Yorkies also love to smile. If your dog is happy and relaxed and wagging his tail when he shows his teeth, smile back!

To help curb excessive barking, learn to acknowledge what your Yorkie is trying to tell you.

animals than live ones. They quickly learn that barking gets attention—even if it's negative attention. In a dog's life, negative attention is better than being bored. So, your dog will bark; you'll say, "Stop it!" The dog will realize it works, so he will do it again; you'll say, "Stop it!" And on it will go.

With some time and attention, you can bring the problem under control. The following are some steps you can take to help curb the barking.

Acknowledge What Your Yorkie Is Telling You

Dogs know they hear things we don't. Like any sensible watchdog, your Yorkie will want to tell you what's going on. If you ignore your dog or just tell him to be quiet, he may decide that you don't understand his message. He's likely to bark louder and more insistently.

Instead of yelling at him to shut up, acknowledge what he's telling you. Go with him to the window and say, "I see the cat; thanks for letting me know." Saying, "Thanks for letting me know" usually will end the cycle, because your dog will know that you heard what he had to say.

Teach Him to Whisper

Your Yorkie can't bark unless he breathes in first. As he's taking that breath, say, "Good whisper!" and give him a treat if one is handy. Within minutes, your pocket-sized pooch will be coming up to you doing silent barks to get your attention. Silent barks are good. Noisy barks are incredibly irritating. Reward the silent barks!

Take Away His Chance to React

If your Yorkie is screeching at squirrels or going ballistic when the mail carrier arrives, sometimes the best solution is to remove him from the scene. Just pick up your Yorkie and hold him where he can't see the squirrel or he doesn't get to snarl at the postal carrier. Chances are, your Yorkie will learn to control himself. It's more fun to watch the squirrel quietly (well, maybe a little whine is fair) than to be taken away from the window.

Yorkies are smart, and your dog will do what gives him the most fun. Screeching at a squirrel is self-rewarding behavior. Learning to control his screech is only worth it to him if the alternative is to miss watching squirrels.

Give Your Dog a Job

Bored Yorkies are noisy Yorkies. They bark at leaves in the wind, the sound of butterfly wings, the breathing of a cat down the street.

Your noisy dog may just need something fun to do. Try going for a walk. Take an obedience or agility class. Teach your dog tricks. Ask your dog to pick up and put away his own toys. Basically, you should become your dog's amusement park on two legs.

Dog Aggression: No Laughing Matter for Your Yorkie

The most dangerous thing your Yorkie can do is to lunge and bark at big dogs. Unfortunately, this is a breed trait. All too often,

If your Yorkie exhibits dog aggression, keep him from coming into contact with other dogs, especially larger ones. You also may want to consult a professional for help.

131

Debarking Surgery

You may have heard about debarking surgery, which reduces your dog's bark to a whisper. Please think twice, and then think again, before considering this for your dog.

Debarking surgery cuts the dog's vocal cords. Not only does this end the barking, but it also makes it impossible for the dog to growl or whine. When you've debarked a dog, you've just eliminated much of his ability to communicate with people and with other dogs.

If your dog has an issue with barking, please train him—don't try to solve the issue with surgery.

Yorkie owners shake their heads and grin at the behavior. They're secretly (and sometimes not so secretly) proud that their tiny little dog isn't afraid of a dog who's 10 or 20 times his size.

The problem is that when your little dog growls and snarls at a big dog, the big dog is likely to respond with a bite. That's what dogs do. If a big dog bites another large dog, the dogs seldom seriously hurt each other. The dogs might require some stitches, but more often than not, no permanent damage is done. At the end of the altercation, they might even be friends. That's not what will happen to your Yorkie. The bite that would leave a small wound on a Labrador will crush your Yorkie's ribs. The nip at the nape of the neck that wouldn't penetrate a Collie's fur will end up in a deathly shake that can snap the neck of a Yorkshire Terrier. If your dog challenges a big dog, it's your fault if the big dog responds like a dog and hurts him.

Rules to Live (Long) By

Don't allow your Yorkie to have prolonged eye contact with, growl at, or snarl at other dogs. Not ever. Period. Instead, teach your dog to look at you (remember that old stand-by of "watch me!") when a larger dog comes by so that your dog can't establish eye contact or get in trouble.

If your dog is likely to be aggressive with another dog, prevent any possible contact. When you see a dog coming, pick your dog up and put him on the side of your body where the other dog won't see him—and where he can't see the other dog.

Don't ever think it's okay that your dog is yapping, snapping, and snarling at another dog. This isn't a small dog acting like a big dog; it's a small dog acting like he's challenging other dogs, and one of them is likely to react. If you secretly admire this trait in your little dog, get over it if you want him to live a long life.

The Hazards of Dog Parks and Doggy Day Care

Nothing could seem more natural than dog parks and doggy day care. Thousands of small-dog lovers take their dogs there every day to give their portable pooches the chance for exercise and friendship with other dogs. This is not a good idea, though. If one dog becomes aggressive toward a smaller, weaker dog, the rest of the dogs might join in the "fun."

If you want your dog to socialize with other dogs, get to know other small-dog owners, and set up a breed-specific playgroup. Lobby your city for a small-dogs-only section in a park, and go to a day care provider who has a separate small-dogs group.

Rough Play

It might seem cute for a Rottweiler or a Golden Retriever to roughhouse with your Yorkie. Inevitably, you'll hear people say, "Isn't it great? They love to play together. The little guy dishes out more than the big one."

This is a recipe for disaster. Watch how your Yorkie is playing with the big dog, and you'll see that he's overly aggressive and tense. The dog is darting in and out. It's highly possible that the game quickly will turn into a quarrel, and the small dog always, always, always loses the quarrel.

In addition, playing so roughly with big dogs makes your Yorkie a poor candidate for playing with dogs his own size. These dogs are so used to overly aggressive play that they don't know how to play politely. The bottom line is that even if your dog is friends with a big dog, they shouldn't play. They can hang out together, and they can go for walks together, but they never should roughhouse.

Growling or Snapping at People

Many Yorkshire Terriers are the poster child for the phrase "Armpit Piranha." These are the little dogs who seem to live in the crook of their doting human's arm, showing a full array of tiny teeth when anyone dares to approach.

Scary Problem Behaviors

Occasionally, a Yorkie will behave in ways that are scary. He'll try to bite you or be so aggressive with other dogs that you don't know what to do. Some Yorkies even have separation anxiety, a disorder that makes them destructive and self-destructive when you are away.

If the problem is larger than dog training, you may need to consult a veterinary behaviorist. These are veterinarians with specialized training in serious problem behaviors. These dedicated professionals will assess the problem behavior and then develop a plan of action to work with the problem, which may include a program of desensitizing the dog to whatever triggers the behavior. The veterinarian also may prescribe medication for your dog, such as anti-anxiety medication, to help him be calm while you work on the behavior change.

To find a veterinary behaviorist, ask your veterinarian for a recommendation. You also can find a listing of veterinary behaviorists at the website of the American College of Veterinary Behaviorists at www.dacvb.net.

There are variations of the Armpit Piranha. For example, lots of Yorkies don't like to share the bed—especially with the spouse of their favorite human. Sometimes it's a chair or a toy. In any event, the dog has decided that no one else is allowed to touch the person or object that he's claimed as his own. By taking control of the situation, you can reclaim your spouse, bed, and other valuables, and your dog will be a happier, calmer family member.

When Your Dog Won't Let People Near You

Small dogs tend to define small territories. Nothing is easier to defend than a lap. As a result, your devoted dog is likely to make very clear boundaries that other people aren't allowed to cross. When your friends and loved ones touch you or come within a certain distance of you, your Yorkie will let them know in a not-too-subtle way that they're supposed to back off. After all, he owns you. Right? Wrong!

You own you. If you put the dog on the ground when he gets pushy, he won't have a territory to defend. He'll stop growling and calm down. Meanwhile, let your Yorkie know that you like people and want him to as well. The best way for him to decide that other people are a good thing is to have them feed him little treats. Carry treats with you on walks, and ask people to feed the dog a little

Teaching your Yorkie to trade what he has for something better will prevent him from becoming possessive of his toys.

morsel. After he's used to accepting treats on the ground, progress to holding him, and ask a friend to offer the treat.

If your dog is good, he gets the treat. If he growls or snarls, put him back on the floor, and have your friend eat the treat. (Be sure to have something that humans like because it's important for the friend to eat and swallow the treat!) Have your friend lick her lips and make a big deal about how wonderful the treat tasted. Wait a day or two, and try again, first treating the dog on the ground and later sitting on your lap. If your friend continues to offer the dog a really yummy treat, sooner or later your Yorkie will figure out that it's better to be a good boy than to miss out on such a delicacy.

Reclaiming Your Bed

It's amazing how much trouble one little dog can cause in a king-sized bed. If your dog is growling at your spouse when he comes into the bedroom, growling when you move in bed, or otherwise making sleep a nightmare, you need to work with him. Plenty of Yorkies happily sleep in their owner's beds. The key to a harmonious bedroom is for the dog to understand it's your bed, and he has the privilege of sleeping there. (Remember, in doggy terms, the lead dog decides who sleeps where, and when.)

To reclaim your bed, teach your dog that you decide when he gets to be on the bed or other furniture. Tell him, "On" and encourage him to come up on the bed. Tell him he's a good boy! Then say, "Off!" and reward him for jumping off. Play the "on" and "off" game regularly to reinforce the fact that you—not the dog—decide when he's on the bed and furniture.

You also should have a reasonable alternative for when your dog isn't behaving. If you have a dog who is territorial about his bed or who has been growling or snapping in any place or at any time during the day, he shouldn't sleep on your bed that night. Be prepared with a reasonable alternative, though. Have a nice, comfy crate set up next to the bed. It should be a nice place to sleep, lined with soft bedding. It's fine to have toys in the crate, as well. When your dog growls, scoop him up and unemotionally put him in the crate. If your dog whines in the crate, ignore him. He's in a nice, comfy spot, and he's in the same room with you, so he knows he's safe and part of the pack. He can earn the privilege of sleeping in your bed tomorrow.

Toy Possessiveness

Remember, Yorkshire Terriers are terriers. All of your dog's larger terrier cousins are also famous for possessiveness. Still, it's important that you don't let your Yorkie morph from sweetheart to Frankenstein when you come near his toys.

The best solution to this problem behavior is to teach your dog that it's not in his best interest to be territorial with his toys. It's easiest to deal with this problem when the dog is a puppy, but the same techniques also can be applied to an adult dog.

Give and Take and Give Toys

Make giving a toy a game. Give the toy to the dog, then take it, and then immediately give it back. Laugh when you do it. Your dog

will learn that you taking a toy from him is not big deal, because he can expect it back.

Teach "Trade"

Give your dog a low-value toy—something that isn't one of his favorites. Then, hold a very high-value treat (such as a piece of steak) and say, "Trade!" Almost always, the dog will be thrilled to trade the low-value toy for the high-value treat. After you've done the trade, you can give the dog his original toy back.

When you play "trade" always make sure you have something in your hand that the dog prefers to whatever he has in his paws. (If he doesn't want to trade, you can just walk away, or better yet, you can eat his high-value treat in front of him, so that he knows that he made the wrong choice by not trading.)

Almost every puppy goes through the "keep-away" phase where he steals something—inevitably something that's dangerous for a puppy—and runs through the house, seemingly laughing at you because you're too slow to catch him. "Trade" is the best response to this not-so-funny game. If your Yorkie knows that "trade!" means he'll be getting the yummiest treat in the household, he's likely to swap whatever dangerous thing he has in his mouth for your first-class treat.

It is important that you always give the dog the best deal in the trade. You want him to come to you when he's stolen a bottle of medicine or a broken shard of glass. He won't willingly give up the "toy" if he doesn't think he's going to get something great in exchange.

Over time, your dog will learn that "trade" is a great game, and that he doesn't need to horde anything.

Training your Yorkie may seem optional—after all, you can just pick him up and carry him if he gets into real trouble. What you'll find, though, is that modern, positive training will enhance your communication with your dog. In addition, it will make his life safer and your life easier. After you've lived with a trained dog, you'll never imagine going back to an untrained one.

ADVANCED TRAINING AND ACTIVITIES

With Your Yorkshire Terrier

ow that your Yorkie knows the basics, think about participating in activities together that are fun for you both. Is your little guy a speed demon? Try agility. Is he a snuggle bunny? Get certified to do animal-assisted therapy. Is he too clever for words? Teach him some tricks to keep that smart little brain of his thinking.

The more you do with your dog, the better bonded both of you will be. You love your dog now, but if you participate in activities together, you will have a depth of communication and understanding that really is magical.

THE AKC CANINE GOOD CITIZEN® TEST

The Canine Good Citizen program evaluates practical, useful skills, such as walking politely on a loose leash, accepting petting and grooming, and staying under control when there's another dog nearby. It demonstrates that your dog is well behaved and listens to you, but it doesn't require precision or years of training. With some basic obedience training and a little leadership from you, any dog has the ability to pass this test.

There can be practical reasons to earn a CGC. In some communities, apartments and condominiums only will allow dogs with CGCs. Earning a CGC is also just plain fun. When you pass, you can send away for a nifty, official certificate that you can frame and hang in the hallway.

When you've passed the test, it's proper to put CGC after your dog's name, for Canine Good Citizen. Most important, though, the title is proof to yourself and others that you and your Yorkie accomplished something together. You have a trained and reliable dog who is an asset to your community. That's something in which you should take pride.

Check with local dog trainers or humane organizations to find Good Citizen testing in your community. Some events are also listed on the AKC's website.

Finding a Competition Trainer

To find a competition trainer, go to a local dog show. Most conformation shows also have an obedience trial. (You can find upcoming shows by going to www.infodog.com.) Watch the people and dogs who are smiling and having a good time, and find out where they train.

Check out the AKC (www.akc.org) and the UKC (www.ukcdogs.com) for information on competition rules and requirements.

Test Requirements

First, the pledge! Before taking the Canine Good Citizen test, owners are asked to sign the Responsible Dog Owners Pledge. You'll agree to care of your dog's health, safety, exercise, and training needs, as well as his quality of life. You'll also agree to show responsibility by doing things such as cleaning up after your dog in public places and never letting your dog infringe on the rights of others. Your Yorkshire Terrier then will be tested on the following:

- Accepting a friendly stranger
- Sitting politely for petting
- Appearance and grooming
- Out for a walk (walking on a loose lead)
- Walking through a crowd
- Sit and down on command—staying in place
- Coming when called
- Reaction to another dog
- Reaction to distraction
- Supervised separation

CONFORMATION: THE GLAMOUR EVENT

When most people think of dog shows and competition, they have one picture in their minds: glamorous dogs strutting around the ring. Certainly, Yorkshire Terriers, with their flowing coats, their saucy style, and their adorable faces, are always crowd favorites.

Yorkies are often very successful show dogs, with the Best of Breed dog frequently placing in group competition. This breed has scaled the top of the show world. In 1978, Ch. Cede Higgins won the Westminster Kennel Club dog show. Ch. Ozmilion Mystification won Crufts—the English equivalent to Westminster—in 1997.

About Conformation

While you might think of dog shows as "beauty contests," they are actually something more than that. The dogs in the ring are compared to the breed standard, which is a blueprint of exactly how the ideal Yorkshire Terrier looks, moves, and even acts.

Show dogs don't just "happen." The dogs who have a chance of doing well at a show are carefully bred for generations. Also, the grooming requirements for a show Yorkie are somewhat mind numbing.

Show dogs are trained to gait (trot smartly at a pace that shows them off to their best advantage), hold still on the table while the judge intimately examines them, and stand still ("stacking") while the judge looks at the profile and stance of the dog.

The judge will look for the dog's breed type: how well he conforms to the standard's description. In the Yorkie ring, that includes details such as the color and texture of the coat and the shape of the eyes and ears.

In addition, the judge will look for structure—the Yorkie's physical soundness, including a level topline, a strong and straight gait, and the dog's general heartiness. The dog is also judged on his temperament, or his personality. A shy or aggressive dog doesn't fit the bill in the show ring. This is also where the indefinable but very real charisma of the top show dogs come in.

The dog who has the whole package—breed type, great structure, and wonderful temperament—is every Yorkie show breeder's ultimate dream.

Showing in the United States

The American Kennel Club sanctions shows all over the country, and you can find one somewhere every weekend of the year.

The primary goal of showing is to become a champion. Male Yorkies who aren't yet champions compete against each other for championship points. They will enter a class that's appropriate for them, such as "Puppy 6 to 9 months," "Bred by Exhibitor," and the catch-all "Open." The winner of each class competes against the other winners of the male classes. The winning male is called the "Winners Dog," and he earns the points toward his championship.

The process is repeated for female dogs. The winning female is called the "Winners Bitch" (females are called "bitches" at shows), and she earns points toward her championship.

To earn a championship, a dog has to acquire a total of 15 points. The Winners Dog and Winners Bitch are awarded between one and five points at a show, depending on how many dogs they defeat. Each dog has to earn at least two majors (shows at which he earns at least three points) on his way to a championship.

It takes an average of 75 entries to result in a championship. Of course, some exceptional dogs earn their titles in as few as three shows, and others may enter well over 100 without ever earning the coveted title.

A conformation show evaluates dogs on how closely they adhere to their breed standard.

Showing in England

Shows in Britain have some interesting differences from those in the United States. Most noticeably, if you see Yorkie judging in the United Kingdom, the dogs will be displayed in line in the show ring on their own individual wooden boxes. These boxes are traditionally draped with a red cover, but sometimes exhibitors will use blue or tartan covers. The dogs are still examined on a table and still gait, much as they do in America, but they otherwise stand on their boxes.

The biggest substantive difference in the shows is how much more difficult it is to gain an English championship than an American one. In English championship shows, only the winning dog and the winning bitch are awarded a challenge certificate (CC). These shows are inevitably very large, and top-winning current champions are vying for the CCs just as the younger, untitled dogs are. It takes three CCs from three separate judges to earn the title of Champion.

If you see a Yorkie with an English championship title, he is a very fine dog, and he beat the best of the best to earn that highly respected title.

Best of Breed, Group Competition, and Best in Show

In both the United States and the United Kingdom, the judge eventually will select a Best of Breed. The winning Yorkie will go on to group competition. Each dog is assigned to one of seven groups: Sporting (called the Gundog Group in England), Hound, Working, Terrier, Toy, Non-Sporting (called Utility in the UK), and Herding (Pastoral in England). Yorkies, of course, are one of the toy breeds.

At the group level, the dogs aren't being compared to each other; they are being compared to how well they match their own breed standards. Thus, if the Yorkshire Terrier comes closer to the Yorkie standard than the Chihuahua comes to the Chihuahua standard, the Yorkie wins. The winner of each group competes for the extraordinary accomplishment of Best in Show.

WORKING YORKIES

Your Yorkie is an intelligent dog who loves a challenge. A wonderful variety of dog sports are available that you and your pint-sized terrier can enjoy and even excel at. Move over, Border Collies—some of those Yorkies will give you a run for your money!

If you want inspiration, look on the Internet. Multiple sites feature Yorkies wearing their pretty red bows as they tear up the competition, while others look ready for action in Schnauzer cuts. Competitors range in size from 4 pounds (1.8 kg) to those who tip the scales well in excess of the breed standard's 7 pounds (3.2 kg). In all cases, these happy dogs and their dedicated owners are clearly having a great time together.

Yorkies can compete in four major performance events: obedience, agility, rally, and tracking. Some less well-known sports also can be a lot of fun, including flyball, freestyle (dancing with dogs), and earthdog events (which Yorkies can do for fun but not for titles).

Here's a taste of the dog sports that your little guy would love to try.

Competitive Obedience

If you think obedience is boring, go watch an obedience trial, and you just might change your mind. This sport, especially with today's positive training methods, is full of tail-wagging fun. It's a happy, bonding experience to show off all the work you've done

What to Wear When You Show

The star of the dog show is the dog, not the handler. However, it is best to wear something that frames the dog when he is on the table being examined by the judge. When Ch. Cede Higgins won the Westminster Kennel Club dog show on Valentine's Day in 1978, his handler, Marlene Lutovsky, famously wore an elegant red dress that highlighted the dog's red and white bow, which in turn brought the eye of the judge to the tiny dog.

Dog shows may be held at county fairgrounds or even farmer's fields, but exhibitors generally wear business attire. Sensible shoes should be worn as well. No one wants to trip!

together and get some titles.

The AKC includes obedience trials at most of its dog shows, and obedience dogs work at the following three levels.

Novice Obedience

At the Novice level, dogs earn a Companion Dog (CD) title. Dogs must heel on- and off-leash in a pattern that includes left turns, right turns, fast pace, slow pace, and halts. You'll heel in a figure eight pattern around two people. The dog must "stand for examination" while the judge touches him lightly on the head, shoulders, and back. He must stay while you leave him, and then when you call him, he should come running and sit in front of you. He should then finish back into the heel position on your left side.

After the individual exercises are complete, all of the dogs from the class come back together into the ring for the long *sit* (one minute) and long *down* (three minutes) while the handlers stand at the other end of the ring.

Your dog must pass these requirements at three different shows (earning a "leg" at each show) to earn his Companion Dog (CD) title.

Open Obedience

At the Open level, dogs earn a Companion Dog Excellent (CDX) title. All Open work is done off-leash. The dog will heel and do a figure eight, as in the Novice Class. On the recall (*come*) exercise,

Kennel Club Sporting Events

The Kennel Club in the United Kingdom sponsors a variety of events for dogs and their owners to enjoy together. For complete listings, rules, and descriptions, please refer to the Kennel Club's website at www.the-kennel-club.org.uk.

Agility

Introduced in 1978 at Crufts, agility is a fun, fast-paced, and interactive sport. The event mainly consists of multiple obstacles on a timed course that a dog must handle. Different classes have varying levels of difficulty.

Flyball

Flyball is an exciting sport introduced at Crufts in 1990. Competition involves a relay race in which several teams compete against each other and the clock. Equipment includes hurdles, a flyball box, backstop board, and balls.

Obedience

Obedience competitions test an owner's and dog's ability to work together as a team. The three types of obedience tests include the Limited Obedience Show, Open Obedience Show, and Championship Obedience Show. Competition becomes successively more difficult with each type of show.

Many Yorkies excel at conformation and events such as obedience and agility.

you will leave the dog, call him, and (on the judge's signal) tell him to down as he's running to you. Then, you will complete the *come* exercise as in Novice. The open class also includes retrieving exercises, and your dog will retrieve a dumbbell across the ring and over a high jump. ("High" is a relative term; your Yorkie's high jump might be 8 inches [20.3 cm] tall, but that's high for a Yorkie!) He also will jump over some low, flat boards. In the long-stay exercises, all the dogs in the class will come back together into the ring for the long *sit* (three minutes) and long *down* (five minutes) while the handlers leave the building (or are taken out of sight).

After passing three times, your dog will earn the Companion Dog Excellent (CDX) title.

Utility

Utility is the most advanced work. All commands are off-leash. Your dog will heel as in Novice, but he must work entirely on hand signals. You'll follow the heeling with a series of signals that require the dog to stand, stay, down, come, and finish. You'll also have leather and metal dumbbells, and your dog must select the items you touch from those you don't. The judge will then put out

145

Teacup Dogs Agility Association

This recently formed organization provides agility competition that is limited to dogs less than 17 inches (43.2 cm) tall. Everything is scaled down for little dogs, with jumps starting at 4 inches (10.2 cm) high and even equipment like seesaws and A-frames scaled down for smaller dogs. For information, check out www.dogagility.org.

three gloves, and your dog must retrieve the glove that you point to. In the "moving stand" exercise, you'll heel and then tell your dog to stay as you continue forward. The judge will touch your dog all over, and then you'll call your dog back to the heel position. The final exercise is the most dramatic: You'll send your dog away from you across the ring, where a solid high jump stands on one side and a bar jump stands on the other. You'll tell the dog to jump over whichever jump the judge designates. Then, you'll send him back to jump the other one.

After passing three times, your dog will earn the respected and coveted Utility Dog (UD) title.

UDX and OTCH

Utility dogs who continue competing and pass both Open and Utility at ten shows after they earn their UD title will earn the Utility Dog Excellent (UDX) title. In these classes, which are limited to dogs with advanced titles, dogs earn points on a designated scale for defeating other dogs. After a dog earns 100 points, he claims the highest title in obedience—Obedience Trial Champion (OTCH).

Agility

Today, agility is America's most popular dog sport, and it truly is an international sport. Whether taking a class just for fun or competing at the national or even international level, Yorkies are great little agility dogs.

Agility is about as much fun as a dog can have with his fur on. Dogs run through an obstacle course, flying over hurdles (set as low as 8 inches [20.3 cm] for small dogs), climbing up A-frames, skipping along dog walks (elevated balance beams), and careening through above-ground tunnels.

Agility Safety

Thousands of dogs take agility classes every day, and the sport is generally very safe. However, it's one of the few dog sports that has the potential for your Yorkie to get a serious injury. Your little dog can hurt himself if he jumps off the top of the A-frame or dog walk, or if he jumps when he isn't warmed up. Also, dogs in agility classes are often very excited and are experiencing a high prey drive, and some bigger animals have been known to chase and hurt small dogs.

Choose an agility class that has safety as its top priority. Don't do anything that doesn't seem safe and sensible for your little Yorkie. Then, have a blast!

Not Registered? Check Out the Indefinite Listing Privilege!

If you have a rescue Yorkie, or if you bought a purebred Yorkie who wasn't registered with the AKC, your neutered pet can still compete in performance events like obedience trials, agility, rally, and tracking. Just go to the AKC's website (www.akc.org) and check out the requirements for the Indefinite Listing Privilege (ILP). This is similar to registering your dog; his ILP number makes him eligible to compete in performance events. To get an ILP number for your Yorkie, you'll need to fill out a form and demonstrate that he is a purebred dog. Once the paperwork is processed, he can compete.

Conformation events do not allow unregistered dogs, even with ILPs, to participate. However, a lot of fun is to be had in the performance events, and your Yorkie will be welcomed, even if he wasn't bred for the show ring.

When competing on a standard course, the dogs go through a course that has a number of contact obstacles (such as A-frames, seesaws, or dog walks), plus items such as weave poles, a pause table (where dogs have to stay to show control), tire jumps, and tunnels. (The Jumpers with Weaves class doesn't have the contact obstacles or the pause table, which slow the dog down. This is a very fast course!)

Dogs progress from the novice level, to open level, to excellent level competition. At each level, the courses are tougher, with more obstacles to navigate and more complicated courses to run.

In the AKC, dogs earn the titles NA and NAJ (Novice Agility and Novice Jumpers with Weaves), OA and OAJ (Open Agility and Open Jumpers with Weaves), AX and AXJ (Excellent Agility and Excellent Jumpers with Weaves), and MX and MXJ (Master Agility and Master Jumpers with Weaves). The very top dogs get the coveted title of MACH. No, this doesn't mean they've exceeded the speed of sound, but these dogs may seem that fast. MACH stands for Master Agility Champion, and this level requires the dog to be both precise and very fast over many trials. Dogs who complete this requirement multiple times attain the title of MACH 1, MACH 2, MACH 3, etc.

Rally Obedience

Imagine the fun of a sports car rally. The drivers follow signs and make twists and turns, and the fastest car to accurately negotiate the course wins the prize. Forget the cars and replace them with dogs, and you have this great new sport.

Judges set up signs that tell the handler what the dog must do. There are 40 different signs that the judge may use. Your dog might have to heel around a set of cones, go fast, lie down, or turn in a 360-degree circle left or a 360-degree circle right.

It's the teamwork that makes the sport so fun. Rally includes the spontaneity of agility without requiring dogs to do a strenuous physical course of jumping and climbing. While it contains obedience skills such as heeling, sitting, and lying down, it's judged less rigorously than traditional obedience competition. Rally competitors are encouraged to talk to their dogs and encourage them along the way. In competition, ties are settled by the fastest time. As a result, dogs and owners go as fast as they can through the course, which makes a dog's tail wag with all the excitement.

It can take years of training for a dog to be ready to compete in agility or traditional obedience. Rally, on the other hand, relies on the combination of a few basic commands that most people learn in dog training classes. Once you learn what the signs mean, even young dogs and inexperienced handlers can enjoy the sport.

Rally Novice is done on-leash. Dogs perform at 10 to 15 stations. The Advanced class is more challenging, because dogs are off-leash and have 12 to 17 stations. At the highest level (Rally Excellent), the course has 15 to 20 stations.

Dogs must pass a course at three different trials to earn a title. The titles are Rally Novice (RN), Rally Advanced (RA), and Rally Excellent (RE). Dogs who have an RE title who pass both the advanced and excellent courses at ten different trials can earn the Rally Advanced Excellent title (RAE).

Tracking

Yorkies may be small, but they have all the instincts of a big dog. That includes an excellent ability to track. The AKC holds tracking events that any purebred can enter, and Yorkies can be just as successful as the big dogs. In fact, because tracking is all about a dog following his nose to find a scent, the dog—not the human—is in charge. Yorkies like this a lot!

Tracking tests are all pass/fail, noncompetitive events that celebrate the instinct of your dog and the bond of trust between the two of you.

Titles include Tracking Dog (TD), Tracking Dog Excellent (TDX), Variable Surface Tracking (VST), and Champion Tracker (CT).

Earthdog

In the sport of earthdog, dogs go through underground tunnels in search of rats. (Don't worry; the rats are safely in cages. The dogs can't hurt the rats, and the rats can't hurt the dogs.) All terrier breeds, Dachshunds, and Silky Terriers are allowed to compete for titles.

Yorkies, who originally were bred to kill rats, aren't allowed to compete for titles in this sport. This is because dog breeds are determined to be eligible for titles in this sport based on the kind of hunting they have historically done, as well as the interest in breed owners in competing in events. Because Yorkies typically didn't follow into burrows after game, and because there has been no sustained, concerted effort by organized Yorkie fanciers to participate in earthdog trials, Yorkies aren't on the list of breeds that can earn titles.

Nonetheless, there may be no activity that makes your Yorkie happier than pursuing rats. Fortunately, many people who put on earthdog events are very open and friendly to people with all breeds of dogs. Usually, above-ground tunnels are available, and some fun introductory exercises to earthdog basics take place at trials. Ask your local earthdog group if your dog can try these fun, non-titling sessions.

Any trick or game that requires physical strain should first include a warmup of running or playing.

Flyball

Flyball is a relay race that consists of four dogs flying over

hurdles, hitting a box that dispenses tennis balls (tiny tennis balls for tiny dogs!), and carrying the tennis balls back to the handler.

Your Yorkie will be in special demand for this sport. Flyball teams are all looking for a small dog (called the "height dog"), because the whole team is permitted to jump over lower hurdles if they have a small dog on their team.

Canine Freestyle

The dog sport that's got everyone talking is canine freestyle, or dancing with dogs. You pick the music and the costumes, and you and your dog dance together. Canine freestyle allows you to select music and tricks that reflect your interests and your dog's abilities, which makes it a ton of fun.

ANIMAL-ASSISTED THERAPY

Many Yorkies are almost magical in their empathy with humans who are suffering. If you have one of those dogs, becoming an animal-assisted therapy team can be one of the most meaningful things you can do. For dogs who like to visit people, there is no more wonderful, joyful activity than bringing a smile to someone's face.

An endless variety of settings is available in which to perform this important work: hospitals, hospices, nursing homes, schools, and libraries. People of all ages and in a variety of physical conditions would love to have your dog visit. You and your dog will find a niche that you both enjoy.

While every dog (and cat, bird, and other creature) who performs this work brings something special to the task, your Yorkie's abilities to sit on beds and laps has a certain charm that a big dog can't match. Some people who are afraid of large dogs enjoy the company of a sweet-faced Yorkie.

Therapy work isn't for every dog, though. Just as every person isn't cut out to be a social worker, every dog isn't cut out to be a therapy dog. People who evaluate therapy dogs estimate that about 25 to 30 percent of trained dogs enjoy this work. No one wants to be visited by a dog who doesn't like them, so if your dog is grouchy with strangers, he may need more training. If he's shy, this probably isn't the activity for him.

If your dog might enjoy this work, try it. You might find it changes your life. (For more information on specific therapy dog

organizations, refer to the Resources section.)

TRICKS AND GAMES

You and your Yorkie might enjoy learning and engaging in a variety of tricks and games together. In fact, the recreational activities you can experience with your Yorkshire Terrier are only limited by your imagination. He'll bond with you more closely when you do activities together, and best of all, you don't even have to leave the condo to have a rousing good time with your little friend.

Just remember that safety is extremely important in whatever you decide to do. It's one thing for a dog to joyfully do something on his own, but it is another to do it because you ask. Dogs less than about a year of age never should be required to jump on command, for example. Any command that takes physical strain should first include a warmup of running or playing to make sure that your pooch doesn't pull a muscle or otherwise injure himself. Always remember to keep your dog's safety as the number-one priority.

Did You Know?

Your Yorkie constantly exhibits behaviors that, when rewarded correctly, can develop into great tricks that will impress your family and friends!

Tricks

Yorkies are clever dogs who love to show off. In fact, your Yorkie will offer behaviors all the time. Any activity that your dog does consistently, you can label and turn into a trick. Catch your dog doing something right, and you can develop unique, enjoyable tricks!

To have your dog perform tricks, just follow the principle of "catching your dog doing something right." When your dog does something fun, say, "Good!" or "Yes!" and reward him with a treat when possible. Soon, your dog will offer the behavior.

The following are a few fun tricks that your Yorkie will enjoy learning.

Please

Ask your dog to sit. Hold the treat about 1 inch (2.54 cm) higher than you would for the *sit*. When your dog reaches up, say, "Good please!" Most dogs will soon sit up if you hold the reward high enough—and directly over their noses. In fact, the majority of dogs learn this trick in one or two sessions!

Your intelligent Yorkie can learn a variety of tricks— with the proper motivation.

Shake

When your dog is very sure of himself on the wave, reach out and gently take his paw and say, "Good shake." Give him a big treat right away so that he thinks that shaking is fun.

Wave

Let your Yorkie see you put a treat in your hand, then wrap the treat in a fist. Hold your fist near your dog's paws. Soon, your dog will start pawing at your fist, basically saying, "Give me that treat!" As soon as his little paws start scratching at your hand, say, "Good wave!" and give him the treat. It takes most dogs just a few minutes to figure out this trick, because it rewards their natural impulse to "dig" for food. If you hold your hand farther away, that "digging" will turn into an arm motion that looks just like a wave!

Games

Your little Yorkie's brain loves getting a workout, so let your dog enjoy some mental stimulation. Fortunately, your pocket-sized pooch can enjoy himself in your home—even if it's a small apartment. Here are a few games that you and your dog can do together without leaving the comforts of home.

Find Me!

With this game, you hide and your dog seeks. If you have a friend or family member to hold the dog while you hide, that's great. If you've taught your dog a reliable stay, that also will give you time to hide.

Start out by "hiding" where your dog can easily find you. Walk just around the corner. Maybe let him see your arm or toe. Then, call him to you and reward him with play and hugs and maybe a treat.

Over time, hide in more and more difficult areas. Try standing behind a door, in the closet, or even crouching in the upstairs bathtub. When you're well hidden, call your dog's name and tell him to come. Keep calling until he finds you, and then reward him with a treat.

This game hones your dog's skills and teaches him to keep track of you.

Where Is It?

Take a favorite toy or a treat, and let your dog see you put it under a washcloth. Ask him, "Where is it?" When he digs and gets it, let him have the treat or play with the toy.

Begin to make the toy or treat just a little hard to find. Put it under your pillow or under the bed. Work up to the point at which you can put the toy or treat anywhere in the room when your dog isn't looking, and he can find it.

Which Hand?

This trick teaches your Yorkie to think with his nose. First, take a favorite treat and put it behind your back. Place it in one hand, and then hold both fists in front of your dog. Ask him, "Which hand?" If he guesses right, he gets the treat. If he guesses wrong, show him what he missed, and say, "Try again!"

Most dogs quickly figure out that they need to sniff to find the yummy treat in the correct hand. Make sure that the game always ends with the dog finding the treat. He needs to know that he wins when he plays this game!

Your Yorkie is a clever, wonderful little dog. The more activities you participate in together, the more fun both of you will have. There is no greater joy than sharing the world together—and training makes that possible.

HEALTH

of Your Yorkshire Terrier

t can be scary thinking about what can go wrong with your Yorkshire Terrier's health. A note of optimism before you read any further: Most Yorkies have a long, full lifespan full of health, vigor, and fun. Thus, while it's important to understand and prevent possible health hazards to your little dog, don't panic when you read the litany of what can go wrong. An informed owner almost always translates into a healthy pup.

This chapter will give you the tools to help your wonderful little buddy live a long, healthy, and vibrant life.

FINDING A VETERINARIAN

After you, there is no more important person in your Yorkie's life than his veterinarian. This is why it's so important to find a veterinarian who is skilled, who will take the time to examine your dog closely, and who will communicate clearly with you.

All veterinarians aren't equal, and all veterinary practices aren't the same. Frankly, some veterinarians are more skilled and knowledgeable than others. At times, the difference is just a matter of style, but remember, if you're in a medical emergency with your dog, you want a veterinarian who understands and reflects your priorities for your dog. You may be making life and death decisions together over the years ahead—take the time now to choose a veterinarian whom you trust to do that with you.

Lots of great sources are available for veterinary referrals. If you bought your Yorkie from a loving, caring breeder, she may be able to suggest an excellent veterinarian. Friends and family members also can suggest veterinarians who have done a good job for them. Also, groomers and dog trainers often know the veterinary community well. No matter who gives you a referral, though, check out the veterinarian before you take your dog there. After all, the veterinarian your neighbor and her Golden Retriever just love might not be a fit for you and your Yorkie. Everyone has a different personality, and the vet your friend thinks is efficient might seem curt to you.

As long as you make an appointment ahead of time, the veterinary staff should be proud to show you their facilities. The entire clinic should be gleaming in its cleanliness.

Veterinarians and other staff should show genuine fondness for animals, talking with them and touching them soothingly. They also should be glad to answer your questions. In addition, it's important to interview your prospective veterinarian. This may seem difficult if you were raised in a household where doctors (and veterinarians have just as much education as medical doctors) were treated as all-knowing and all-powerful. However, you owe it to the little life entrusted in your care to find the best doctor for him. Asking questions now can save misery later on. You aren't insulting the veterinarian with your questions, you are just trying to find the right fit for you and your dog.

Ten Questions to Ask a Prospective Veterinarian

The following are some examples of questions you may want to consider asking any prospective veterinarian:

- *How many Yorkshire Terriers or other toy dogs do you regularly treat?* There is an art to caring for a 3- (1.4 kg) or 6-pound (2.7 kg) dog that veterinarians who usually only treat Labradors or horses may not develop.
- *Are you active in local or national veterinary associations?* These associations are the best way for veterinarians to keep current on the latest developments in veterinary medicine.
- *What arrangements do you make for hours when your clinic is closed?* Some veterinarians are on call during off hours. Increasingly, emergency veterinary clinics are available to take animals when other veterinary offices are closed.
- *What kind of anesthesia do you use when you perform surgery?* A Yorkie can be sensitive to anesthesia. Your veterinarian should be using one of the modern, safer gas anesthetics, such as isoflurane, which are much safer than the old-fashioned intravenous anesthetics.
- *What kind of monitoring equipment is in place during surgery?* Dogs are put under anesthesia frequently for procedures like spaying or neutering, teeth cleaning, and x-rays. It's important that your veterinarian has continuous monitoring for heart functions, as well as other vital functions.
- *Do you have certified veterinary technicians on your staff?* Some veterinarians save money by having untrained veterinary assistants help during surgery. The best veterinarians use certified veterinary technicians. These trained professionals

complete a rigorous two-year course of study (there are some programs that are four-year degrees) that is equivalent to a nursing degree. Your pet is safer if he is benefiting from the skills of a trained technician during surgery rather than an untrained assistant. Having high-quality staff is a sign of a high-quality veterinarian.

- *How long have the veterinarians on the staff worked here?* Most veterinary hospitals are owned by one veterinarian and also have one or more other veterinarians working on staff. A constant turnover of veterinarians is a warning sign that this clinic isn't a happy place. Of course, young veterinarians often leave a clinic once they've saved up enough money to open their own practices. Others may decide to move to another area, or go to a clinic with a specialty that's of interest to them. Thus, not all turnover is bad. Still, if most veterinarians on staff have just been there a year or two, ask why.

- *Are you certified by the American Animal Hospital Association (AAHA)?* Trained consultants regularly visit these veterinary hospitals to ensure compliance with AAHA's standards for services and facilities. Think of it as the "Good Housekeeping Seal of Approval" for veterinary offices. Although some excellent veterinary hospitals don't choose to participate in the organization, certification is one good indication that the clinic is committed to quality veterinary care.

- *How much time do you schedule for a routine appointment?* Some veterinarians schedule as little as ten minutes for a routine appointment, while others schedule as much as a half hour. If you want a veterinarian who is going to take the time to listen to your questions and explain your dog's health issues thoroughly to you, it won't happen in a ten-minute visit.

- *How often do you refer animals to specialty clinics?* In most parts of the country, the days of the old country vet who did just about everything from delivering calves to bandaging a pet lizard's tail are long gone. With increased medical technology, specialists are available who are just as knowledgeable as human medical specialists in areas such as heart surgery, neurology, allergies, ophthalmology, oncology, and surgery. If you want the very best care for the life of your Yorkie, look for a veterinarian who refers cases to the experts when more expertise can help your dog. Keep in mind that the best veterinarian in the world won't do your Yorkie much good if she doesn't communicate well. If the veterinarian can't speak clearly with you during a routine office visit, think how difficult communication will be during the course of a long illness.

Remember, too, that the least expensive veterinarian usually isn't the best veterinarian. The most sophisticated equipment, the most qualified staff, on-going training—none of it is cheap. When your Yorkie is sick and needs help, you'll want to know in your heart that he's getting the very best care available.

Many veterinary clinics have a number of veterinarians who practice at the facility. Select one as your primary veterinarian and always ask for her when you're making nonemergency appointments for your Yorkie. Your dog will benefit from having one veterinarian who becomes familiar with him and can notice subtle changes over time.

Teaching Your Yorkie to Like His Veterinarian

The most important hour your dog spends every year is his annual checkup with the veterinarian. This is the time when your dog's doctor can check for problems such as collapsed tracheas, luxating patellas, diseases of aging, and generally help your dog live for many long, happy years.

Sadly, if your dog is wriggling and squirming or snarling and snapping, your veterinarian can't do her job. One vet put it this way, "It's like taking your car to a mechanic, and telling him that something is wrong with the car and he needs to fix it—but he can't touch the car."

Practice Touching Your Dog all Over

One of the biggest problems at the veterinarian's office is that many dogs don't want anyone looking at their teeth or inside their mouths. Make sure that touching your Yorkie's muzzle and lips is part of his regular routine.

Say, "Lips," and then touch his lips and give him a treat. When this is routine for him, pull up his lips and say, "Teeth." The more you can practice gently opening your dog's mouth, the better prepared your dog will be to accept potentially lifesaving medical treatment.

You also can prepare your Yorkie to deal with a stethoscope. This contraption is very scary to a dog who doesn't see one

Trust Your Gut

If you visit a prospective vet's office and don't get a good feeling about it for whatever reason, keep looking. Your vet is going to be a very important person in your Yorkie's life, and you absolutely must be comfortable trusting your dog to her care.

regularly. To prepare him, touch your dog with a variety of objects, like plastic bags, spoons, and crinkled up aluminum foil, so it isn't upsetting to him to feel the cold metal and plastic of the stethoscope.

Make the Veterinarian's Office a Fun Destination

Take your Yorkie to the veterinarian, feed him cookies, and go home. If someone in a white coat is available, ask that person to give the dog some treats, too. As your dog becomes more comfortable in the vet's office, ask your pooch to perform a *sit* and *down*, and reward him for his good behavior. Basic obedience exercises, like the *sit*, *stay*, and *down*, help your veterinarian tremendously.

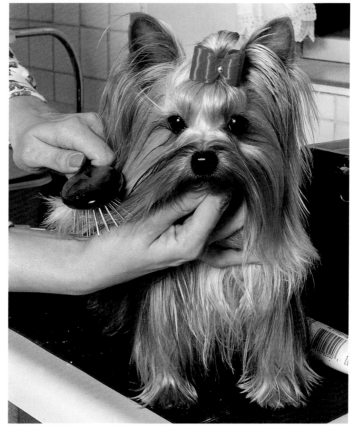

To help your Yorkie learn to like the vet, practice touching him all over in a variety of situations.

Make appointments fun, too. Bring your dog's favorite treat and give him his "cookies" while your veterinarian is examining him. (Of course, check with your veterinarian that treats are appropriate; for example, it's important that food is withheld prior to your dog undergoing surgery, even something like a simple teeth cleaning.) After a few visits, your Yorkie is likely to yip with joy when you come near the vet's office.

If Your Dog Might Be Aggressive, Plan Ahead

Can you imagine what it must be like to be a veterinarian and have a dog suddenly lunge and bite? Now, imagine how upset you would be if the person with the dog said, "Oh, he just does that!"

Even though your dog is small, his bite still can hurt and even injure the veterinarian and veterinary staff. Be respectful of the difficult job that veterinarians perform. If your dog might bite, let

The Annual Vet Visit

Don't skimp on money by skipping annual visits to your veterinarian. Even if your Yorkie is healthy and doesn't need a teeth cleaning, and you've decided he doesn't need a vaccine booster, he still needs to see the veterinarian.

Remember, a year in the life of a dog is roughly equivalent to seven human years. Even those of us who don't like doctors go more often than that. The annual exam is the chance to catch a disease before it becomes serious. Your veterinarian should listen to your dog's heart and lungs, examine his eyes, check for patella luxation (in which she'll gently and skillfully make sure your dog's kneecap fits properly on his leg), feel his skin for lumps and bumps, compare his weight to what it was a year before, and check to see that he is generally healthy.

Going for a yearly veterinary examination even may save you money in the long run, because you'll catch problems early, before they become serious.

the veterinary staff know ahead of time so that they can deal with the situation.

If your dog needs to be muzzled when he goes to the veterinarian, practice using a muzzle at home so that it won't add to the dog's stress.

Dealing With Painful or Sensitive Areas

Some dogs have chronic health problems that require regular medical checkups. Be sure to acclimate the dog to being touched on those sensitive areas. At the same time, be sure not to only be touching that part of his body, or he'll begin to worry about it. Thus, if your dog has a paw that needs some sort of regular attention, check his paw (and say, "Good foot!" when you do) and then check out his ears, tail, or teeth. Handling a problem area should be routine and comfortable for your Yorkie—not scary.

THE WELL-DOG VISIT

Within 48 hours of bringing your new Yorkshire Terrier home, take him to your veterinarian for a well-pet visit. Even if your dog doesn't have any shots due, it's important for your veterinarian to give him a comprehensive medical examination right away.

Your veterinarian will listen to your new dog's heart and lungs, palpate his tummy, and look for abnormalities in his eyes. She will inspect his teeth and gums and look for swelling in his glands. Your veterinarian also will want you to bring in a stool sample to check for worms. She even may do a blood test, especially if you have an older dog or have adopted a rescue dog. If there is a health problem with your new Yorkie, this is the time to spot it.

A well-pet exam is a great time to see if this is really the right veterinarian for you. Especially for little dogs, the hubbub and newness of a veterinarian's office can be intimidating. Look for a veterinarian who holds your Yorkie gently and talks to him sweetly. You can ask the veterinarian to give your dog treats, so that your new pooch learns that veterinarians are fun and wonderful humans, and vet offices are fun places to be. The happy rapport your dog develops from that first visit will go a long way toward making shots, spaying or neutering, and other necessary veterinary procedures during his lifetime far less traumatic.

A note of caution at the vet's office: Remember, this is where people bring their sick animals. While veterinarians clean and disinfect their offices scrupulously, it's always a good idea to hold your dog on your lap in the waiting area, especially if you have a puppy who hasn't completed his vaccinations yet.

VACCINES: PROTECTION AND CONTROVERSY

Vaccines can prevent diseases that can cause your Yorkie to become seriously ill. Canine distemper used to rage through kennels, shelters, and neighborhoods, and parvo killed countless puppies and adult dogs. If you purchase a puppy from a responsible source and then correctly vaccinate your dog, you will not have to worry about these diseases.

The old advice used to be that your dog needed vaccinations against several diseases as a puppy, and that your adult dog should get booster shots every year. The old thinking was that a vaccine wasn't going to hurt anything, and it was better to vaccinate for everything (and repeat the vaccinations every year) than to risk the health of a dog. Then, veterinarians started noticing some problems in cats. In 1998, concerns about increased rates of a certain kind of cancer in cats at vaccine-injection sites were reported in the *Journal of the American Veterinary Medical Association*. Subsequent studies have demonstrated that between 1 in 1,000 and 1 in 10,000 cats will develop cancer from receiving vaccines.

Those discoveries in cats underscored the fact that vaccines aren't entirely harmless. They are powerful agents going into your Yorkie's body. While dogs don't seem to have vaccine-related cancers, some reports suggest that certain kinds of health problems, such as allergies, may be exacerbated by overvaccinating.

Leptospirosis Vaccines

If your veterinarian recommends a vaccination against leptospirosis, be sure you have discussed this vaccine in-depth. This disease is a serious one, and animals who spend time in forested areas are most likely to be exposed to it. However, it is one of the vaccines that has had the most frequent reports of severe anaphylactic shock, which means your dog could stop breathing and could even die. The University of California at Davis School of Veterinary Medicine says that the incidence of severe reactions are most common in puppies and small-breed dogs. They conclude that "a careful risk-benefit analysis is recommended before considering vaccination of small-breed dogs at risk of exposure to leptospires."

Today's pet lovers look for a happy medium: ensuring that their dogs are well protected but not overvaccinated. Frankly, where to draw that line is still being studied by the veterinary community. The problem is that, as of now, no one knows for sure how long a vaccine provides immunity. Currently, studies are underway to determine how long a vaccination will protect your dog against disease, so in the future, recommended vaccine protocols may change.

The following is being recommended by most veterinary schools throughout the country at this time.

The Core Vaccines: Every Puppy Needs Them

No controversy surrounds the basics: All puppies need core immunizations against the most deadly diseases. A puppy's mother's milk gives him immunity for the first several weeks of his life (assuming she is healthy and was given the proper vaccinations). After your puppy is weaned, vaccinations give your dog his own immunity.

Some vaccines are necessary to prevent your Yorkie from contracting a harmful or fatal disease.

Puppy vaccines are given in a series between the ages of about

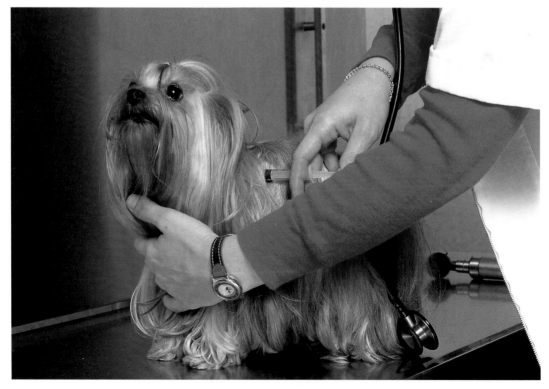

six weeks and four months. Although many people assume that these shots gradually build up a puppy's immunity, this is not the case. A puppy who still has temporary immunity from his mother's milk won't receive immunity from a vaccination. The problem is that it is impossible to know exactly when the mother's temporary immunity will wear off, so the puppy vaccines are repeated until the age of four months.

Every puppy should have these core vaccinations: rabies, parvovirus, distemper, and adenovirus-2 (which also protects against canine infectious hepatitis). These diseases are still widespread, and they can be deadly if the animal comes down with them. Vaccines for these diseases have a low likelihood of side effects.

The Optional Vaccines: Decide Based on the Situation

Other diseases are less widespread, and whether a vaccine's benefits outweigh the risk depends on where you live and your Yorkie's lifestyle. For example, Lyme disease is common in some areas of the United States and not in others, so your vet may not recommend this vaccine. Leptospirosis is a concern in some areas, but the disease hasn't been reported for decades in other parts of the United States. Bordetella (kennel cough) is a flu-like illness that your dog may be exposed to if you board him or take him to dog shows, but he may not be in danger if you don't go places with large numbers of other dogs. If your veterinarian recommends these vaccines, be sure to discuss the reasons why your Yorkie should—or shouldn't—have them.

The Booster Dilemma

Most veterinary schools currently recommend that puppies receive their initial vaccines and then be given boosters a year later. After that, most recommend giving a booster every third year. To keep the level of vaccines as low as possible, many veterinarians set up a routine to give a rabies booster one year, a distemper booster the next, and a parvo booster the following year, and then back to rabies. Boosters of any kind are still controversial, and it is possible that in future years fewer or maybe even no boosters will be given.

The choices about which diseases to vaccinate against and how often to give boosters are important ones for the well-being of your

What to Vaccinate Against

Your dog will require his core vaccinations in order to be protected against rabies and other deadly diseases. Whether he should receive any other vaccines (such as for Lyme disease or leptospirosis) is dependent on several factors. Consult your veterinarian about the vaccinations your Yorkie should receive.

Yorkie. A dedicated, knowledgeable veterinarian who keeps up on the latest research about vaccine protocols is the very best defense for keeping your dog safe.

Vaccinations: Don't Try This at Home

Open up pet supply catalogs or go to hundreds of Internet sites, and you can see vaccines for sale. It's tempting to think about saving some money in giving your Yorkie vaccines at home, but this can be a serious mistake.

For one thing, it is increasingly recognized that vaccines aren't "one size fits all" medications. Many vaccines come in different forms. Do you choose a modified live vaccine or a killed version? Depending on the age, size, and general health of your Yorkie, the right choice might vary. In addition, depending on these same factors, your veterinarian might space out your dog's vaccinations rather than give him a single multivirus vaccine.

Also, many veterinarians believe that not all vaccine brands have the same quality. Bulk vaccines are cheaper, but most veterinarians agree that single-shot packages provide better quality control and have less chance of adverse side effects.

All of these factors are important health decisions that should be made with a knowledgeable, caring, helpful professional who knows the needs of your dog. Vaccinations at a veterinarian's office aren't extremely expensive, and they are worth every dime you pay.

INTERNAL PARASITES

A whole universe of creatures—from microscopic to pretty darn big—can live in your Yorkie's intestines, blood, or heart. Left untreated, these creatures can kill your dog. Happily, modern medicine has made it easy to either prevent or treat most kinds of worm infestations. Keeping a sharp eye on your dog and getting medical help as soon as you notice something wrong will ensure that these pests are just a minor inconvenience in your dog's life.

Signs of worms include:
- A round potbelly on an otherwise thin dog
- Diarrhea
- Blood in stools
- Dull coat
- Lack of energy, listlessness
- Visible worms in the dog's feces or vomit

If you see any of these signs, call your veterinarian. She may ask you to bring in a stool sample so that she can check for microscopic signs of worms.

Roundworms

Many puppies, even from good breeders, are born with roundworms. Even if your dog's mom didn't show any signs of worms, roundworms live in a dormant state in the muscles of a dog. When a female becomes pregnant, hormones cause the dormant roundworm larvae to migrate from her muscles into the puppies and the milk supply.

Although most cases of roundworms aren't life threatening, a heavy infestation can cause vomiting, diarrhea, and even death.

When you take your puppy to the veterinarian for routine vaccines and other visits, bring a stool sample so that your vet can check for roundworms.

Hookworms and Whipworms

Puppies can pick up hookworms when they are playing in a park or going on an outing. They also can contract hookworms while still with their mothers, although they cannot actually contract them from their mothers. Left untreated, a hookworm (which is a bloodsucker that lives in your dog's intestines) can kill a little Yorkie in a matter of a few weeks.

Whipworms are picked up in the environment. (A whipworm egg can live in the soil for years.) If your dog sniffs the feces of an infected dog, or if he munches on something in infected soil, he can pick up a whipworm. Like hookworms, whipworms live in your dog's intestines. Although whipworms are unlikely to kill a dog, they can cause serious inflammation to the intestinal lining, causing colitis and other intestinal problems. A sign of whipworms is diarrhea with blood or mucus.

Both hookworms and whipworms respond well to medication that your veterinarian can prescribe. Over-the-counter worm medications that you may see at the store do not treat these worms—this is a job for your veterinarian.

Did You Know?

Most puppies are born with roundworms, or contract them from their mother's milk after birth, even if the mother showed no signs of an infestation.

Tapeworms

Tapeworms are passed into your dog's system when he swallows a flea, and the worm robs your dog of the nutrients he

Check your dog for fleas and ticks after he has been playing outdoors.

needs to live. In an extreme case, if left untreated, your dog could starve to death, because the tapeworm would be robbing him of all his nutrition. Happily, tapeworms are easy to notice. (You'll see segments of the worm that look like grains of rice in your dog's feces.) They are also easily and effectively treated with a prescription from your veterinarian.

Heartworms

Heartworms depend on dogs and mosquitoes to live. These ugly worms, which look a bit like spaghetti, live in a dog's heart and lungs. While other internal parasites usually aren't fatal in an adult, healthy dog, heartworms are, because these worms block the flow of blood to parts of a dog's lungs, which forces the heart to work harder. Eventually, the dog will develop congestive heart failure. Symptoms include loss of energy, a cough, a heart murmur, difficulty breathing, and eventually, collapse.

Years ago, heartworms were a problem for dogs in the southeastern part of the United States. Now the problem has spread to virtually all corners of the country, and your Yorkie should be on a heartworm preventive medication. The medications have low dangers of side effects in Yorkies. Talk with your veterinarian about selecting a brand that allows for especially tiny doses for your tiny dog; some brands have a special dose for dogs from 2 pounds (0.9 kgs) to 10 pounds (4.5 kgs). Some heartworm preventatives also help prevent infestations of whipworms, hookworms, and roundworms.

Don't wait until your Yorkie has become infested to treat him. The treatment for a case of heartworms is dangerous and difficult, so the best defense against these horrible parasites is your monthly heartworm preventative.

What to Do for Internal Parasites

General danger signs to watch for in a dog infested with internal parasites include a round tummy (not just the tummy of a well-fed pup, but one that is round when the rest of the dog is thin), a dull or thin coat, and diarrhea. Even if no physical signs are present, you still should bring a stool sample to check for worms during your puppy's regular visits to the vet.

A lot of over-the-counter medications are available for worms— don't use them. The modern medications that your veterinarian will prescribe are much easier on your dog's system, and they are safer than most of what you can find in stores.

Your veterinarian probably will ask you to keep bringing in stool samples for a while after your dog has been cleared of the worms, and you should follow her instructions. All worms have a life cycle, and reinfestation is always possible. To keep your little dog safe, follow to the letter exactly what your veterinarian asks you to do.

EXTERNAL PARASITES

Creepy crawlies aren't limited to the worms that can invade your dog's insides. In fact, some external bugs want your Yorkie's blood. Fleas and ticks are two of the most common. Don't panic when you see them, but do treat them.

Fleas

Fleas are tiny bugs that you might not even notice when the infestation begins. If your Yorkie starts biting at his skin, there's a good chance that he is suffering from fleas. It's possible that you may not see the little bugs on your dog, because he has a dark coat. If you run a wet paper towel on his coat, though, you might see bits of blood, because flea "dirt" (flea feces) is comprised primarily of dried blood. If you place your dog on a white sheet while you groom him, you'll also be able to notice the dark flakes of flea "dirt" if he has fleas.

Pyometra

Unspayed females can develop pyometra, a painful, dangerous, and sometimes fatal uterine infection.

Fleas can be a major health hazard for your Yorkie. A bad flea infestation can kill a puppy, because he will lose too much blood to survive. Even a single flea can carry tapeworms and can cause allergies in your little guy.

What to Do for Fleas

If your dog truly only has just one or two fleas that he picked up when he was playing with another dog, bathe him thoroughly with his regular shampoo and keep a close eye on him. You might be able to end the problem without chemicals. More likely than not, though, you'll need help. Visit your veterinarian right away and ask for a recommendation. Many modern prescriptive flea-killing agents have very low toxicity and come in doses appropriate for toy-sized dogs.

Use caution when considering over-the-counter flea remedies for your dog. Many of these products are highly toxic and will do more harm than the fleas. Consult with your veterinarian before making any over-the-counter purchase.

Ticks

Ticks can carry deadly diseases, including Lyme disease and Rocky Mountain Spotted Fever, as well as a condition called "tick paralysis," which can cause paralysis and death in a dog. Therefore, it's important to check your Yorkie after you've been out walking in grassy or wooded areas.

Ticks look very different before and after a meal. Before a meal, they are small; some aren't much bigger than a flea. They have hard shells. After feeding on your dog's blood, they swell to several times their original size.

When searching for ticks, pay special attention to your Yorkie's head, ears, neck, and toes. Also, take a good look at places where body parts come together, like elbows.

What to Do for Ticks

If you see a tick on your Yorkie, don't panic—take action. If you're near a veterinary hospital, the easiest solution is to head on in and have them take the creepy thing off your dog. Vets deal regularly with ticks, and they will be able to take it out quickly and efficiently.

If you are not near a vet, you can remove the tick yourself.

Ticks bury their heads in the body of your dog, so using a pair of tweezers, clamp down as close to the head of the tick as you can and pull it straight out. Try to keep the tick intact. If you leave the head in your dog's body, take the dog to a veterinarian as soon as is practical. Then, wash the spot thoroughly with soap and water, and apply an antibacterial ointment. Also, wash your own hands very thoroughly, because many diseases that ticks carry affect humans as well as dogs. (If you can safely keep the tick, that might help your veterinarian to diagnose any illness that your Yorkie might develop.)

Watch your dog for signs of illness for the next couple of weeks. If he develops a fever, vomits, is wobbly on his feet, is lethargic, or shows other symptoms, take him to your veterinarian right away.

In areas with heavy tick infestations, it may be a good idea to talk with your veterinarian about having your dog vaccinated against Lyme disease.

Unless you plan to breed or show your Yorkie, he or she should be neutered.

NEUTERING YOUR YORKIE

Unless you plan to breed show dogs, it is important to neuter

Secondhand Smoke

If you need another reason to quit smoking, here's a good one: Secondhand smoke makes the condition of having a collapsed trachea worse, because the lining of the trachea already tends to be inflamed from the disease, and secondhand smoke exacerbates the problem.

your pet Yorkie. Here are some good reasons why:

- *Your dog will live longer.* Breast, ovarian, and testicular cancer are leading killers among dogs. The American Kennel Club Canine Health Foundation reports that the incidence of mammary tumors in female dogs is almost three times higher than it is in human women, and most canine mammary tumors are malignant! A female dog who hasn't been spayed by the time she is two years old has a 50 times greater risk of mammary tumors than a dog who has been spayed before she comes into her first heat cycle.

  Cancer isn't the only health risk. Male dogs who haven't been castrated are much more likely to roam, and little Yorkies are surprisingly clever at dashing through doors. Roaming dogs are in very serious danger of being injured or killed by cars, other animals, and dog fights. Plus, any Yorkie on the street is a tempting creature for someone to "rescue" and keep as a pet.

- *Your carpets will thank you.* Yorkie males are notorious leg lifters. Male dogs who are neutered as puppies are the least likely to mark their territories. Even later neutering can help your carpet. One study found that about 25 percent of male dogs stop almost all of their territorial marking after neutering, and about 60 percent reduce their marking behavior by more than half.

- *Having a litter of puppies is financially and emotionally draining.* With the soaring popularity of Yorkshire Terriers, it's easy to envision a fat profit from a litter of puppies. The reality is very different.

  Yorkies have small litters—often only two or three puppies. Even a healthy female with a normal pregnancy can rack up medical expenses, including the cost of checkups (which may include ultrasounds and blood tests), testing for progressive retinal atrophy, and a stud fee, among other expenses. To make matters worse, Yorkies are little dogs, and it's easy for them to run into complications during pregnancy and delivery. Some reports suggest that 20 percent of Yorkie pregnancies require caesarean sections. Sadly, it's inevitable that some puppies die, even with the best of care and attention.

  In the "old days," people wanted to teach their children about the miracle of birth, so they'd have a litter of puppies. Today, we know it's better to teach children lessons of compassion and responsibility. To help your children to grow to be loving,

When Your Yorkie Needs Surgery or Dental Work

Almost every dog will be spayed or castrated, so surgery is a fact of life for dogs. Also, an annual teeth cleaning means your dog will have to undergo anesthesia. Here is a checklist of things to consider when your dog will be getting surgery or dental work:

- Request pre-anesthetic blood work. This is a simple blood test before your dog is put under anesthesia. It is worth the money to have this testing done, especially for Yorkies. Because Yorkies can have undetected liver disease, surgery can be a little riskier for them than for other dogs. A simple blood test will check for liver disease and other problems, and you can go into the surgery knowing that your dog has a clean bill of health and should do just fine.

- Ask what kind of monitoring the veterinarian uses during surgery. Your veterinarian should be monitoring your dog for heart functions and other vital signs, just like humans are monitored when they have surgery. If your veterinarian doesn't do this, select a different veterinarian.

- If your dog has had surgery, request pain medication. Veterinarians used to believe that pain helped an animal know it was important to stay quiet, and they didn't prescribe pain medication. Studies have proven that this thinking was wrong. Animals recover more quickly if they are given pain medication, just as humans do. The American Veterinary Medical Association now has a statement in favor of pain medication after surgery. Talk with your veterinarian about what is the best type and dose of pain medication for your pet, and be sure to follow the exact dosage.

empathetic, kind people, teach them the importance of spaying and neutering animals, as well as the value of supporting responsible rescue organizations.

If you are considering becoming a breeder, don't rush into the decision to breed a specific dog. The future of Yorkshire Terriers lies in the hands of the people who breed them. Purchase breeding stock from the very best lines, and select dogs with outstanding temperament, health, structure, and appearance. Go to seminars on the breed and read the dozens of books about good breeding practices. Develop mentors in the breed so that you're benefiting from the experience of people who know the breed well.

Put breed health as your top priority. Have all of your dogs screened for progressive retinal atrophy (PRA), and don't breed a dog who has luxating patellas, liver disease, Legg-Calve-Perthes disease, or whose close relatives have a history of those problems. Don't forget to factor in time to socialize the puppies properly.

Only breed if you are committed to protecting and preserving the well-being of this delightful breed. People who breed with those values in mind, though, will seldom make a profit on a litter.

When Should I Neuter My Yorkie?

Talk with your veterinarian about the best time for this

One sign of a liver shunt is a dog who doesn't grow.

operation. Increasingly, very early neutering has become a well-accepted alternative. If a puppy is at least 2 pounds (0.9 kgs) and healthy, your veterinarian might suggest performing the operation as soon as possible. Other veterinarians like to wait until a Yorkshire Terrier is a little older—up to about six months. With toy breeds, some veterinarians wait until the dog's permanent teeth are in so they can pull any puppy teeth that didn't come out on their own.

For the health of your female dog, it is advisable that she be spayed before she comes into her first heat cycle, which usually occurs when she's about 5 to 7 months of age. Going through heat cycles will increase her chance of getting dangerous mammary tumors.

The following are some common questions that Yorkie owners have about neutering their pets:

1. *How dangerous is the operation, and how long will it take my dog to recover?*

   It is understandably scary to take your healthy puppy in to the veterinarian's office and know that he is going to have surgery. It's normal to worry.

   Happily, with today's modern anesthetics and pre-operation blood screening to rule out illness, it's extremely safe to have your dog neutered. Although all operations have some risk, the odds of a long, healthy life for your Yorkie are much better if your pet is neutered than if you keep your Yorkie intact. You are doing the right thing to neuter your pet!

   Recovery time is usually only a couple of days. Your biggest problem will probably be to keep your Yorkie as quiet and restrained during the few days after surgery as your veterinarian wants you to.

2. *What if my male Yorkie was born with only one testicle—or none?*
Your male Yorkie has both testicles somewhere. A puppy's testicles normally descend from his abdomen into his scrotum. However, it's fairly common for testicles in male toy dogs to fail to descend. It's extremely important for these dogs to be neutered. This is because it is much more common for retained testicles to become cancerous, so your veterinarian will need to remove any undescended testicles. This requires your veterinarian to open up his abdomen, meaning the scope of the surgery is more like spaying than a castration. In fact, this is a slightly more serious surgery than a neuter, and it will take a few days of recovery time. It's still much healthier for a dog to go through this more extensive surgery than to face the potential increased risk of cancer from an undescended testicle, though. Dogs with one descended testicle never should be bred, because this is a hereditary problem.

3. *Will neutering make my dog fat or change his charming personality?*
Of course not. Dogs get fat because they eat too much and exercise too little—not because they are neutered. And your terrific little dog will be just the same, except male dogs will be less likely to lift a leg and less likely to become a door dasher.

YORKIE-SPECIFIC HEALTH ISSUES

Every breed of dog has some health problems. Yorkies, although generally healthy, do have some serious health problems that can affect their happiness and even drastically shorten their lives. It is best to know about these diseases before you purchase a dog. If you already have your Yorkie (or more than one!), be aware of these problems so that you can catch them early if they arise.

The following conditions occur in a number of breeds. However, Yorkies suffer from them at a higher rate than many other breeds, so they bear special attention.

Collapsed Trachea

The trachea, also called the windpipe, is the tube that connects your dog's lungs to his mouth and nose. Unfortunately, some Yorkies have a condition called a collapsing trachea, in which the top of the trachea flattens out and even collapses. This can make

Liver Shunt Risk

Yorkshire Terriers are almost 36 times more likely to develop shunts than all other breeds combined.

breathing difficult, and the condition can be fatal.

Signs

Signs of a collapsed trachea include coughing (especially with a honking sound) breathing hard, or struggling for breath. Often, the first symptom of a tracheal collapse is your dog breathing very hard after exercising.

What It Isn't—Reverse Sneezing

"Reverse sneezing" is a common condition in toy dogs that is often confused with tracheal collapse. Happily, reverse sneezing is not a serious problem. When your Yorkie reverse sneezes, he will stick his head and nose forward and make snorting sounds. Some people call it "snorkeling." It is most likely to come at stressful times, but sometimes dogs snorkel for no apparent reason. If your Yorkie starts reverse sneezing, you can gently hold your hand on your dog's muzzle or open his mouth with your fingers so that he breaths through his mouth, which will usually stop the incident. Sometimes distracting him helps—like it helps end a case of the hiccups. No one knows what causes reverse sneezing, but it isn't harmful, and you don't need to take your dog to the veterinarian. If your dog is struggling for breath, it is not reverse sneezing and may be sign of a tracheal collapse

Treatment

If your dog is experiencing any of the signs of tracheal collapse, see your vet immediately. She may prescribe anti-inflammatory drugs and cough suppressants, which sometimes help. In more severe cases, surgery may be recommended. If your Yorkie is overweight, a diet almost certainly will help reduce the symptoms of the problem.

Legg-Calve-Perthes Disease

Dogs with Legg-Calve-Perthes disease have reduced blood flow to their hip joints. This causes sections of the bone to die, leaving the joint surface roughened and irregular. It can affect one back leg or both. This condition is painful for your dog, making something as simple as walking quite difficult.

Legg-Calve-Perthes disease usually appears when your puppy is from 4 to 12 months old. There are some arguments about what causes the problem—some Yorkie breeders say it is a heredity condition, while others say that injury to the joint causes the disease. (Because some breeds have a much higher incidence of this condition than others, some sort of hereditary component is almost surely contributory to the problem.)

Signs

The main symptom of this disease is pain in the dog's hips and lameness. It commonly develops when a dog is young (usually between the ages of 3 and 13 months), so if your youngster is limping or seems sensitive around his hip area, it's important to take him in for a veterinary examination.

Treatment

If your dog is limping, he must be seen by your veterinarian right away. The severity of this disease ranges from mild to very serious. Sometimes a period of crate rest (no walking, running, or jumping) and pain management are enough to help your Yorkie through a less severe case. In other cases, surgery to remove the diseased part of the bone is the only relief for your dog.

If your vet recommends surgery, your dog won't be in any pain afterward. Sometimes the surgery on the bone will leave one leg a bit shorter than the other, so the dog may limp slightly, but he'll be able to painlessly and happily scamper throughout a long and healthy life. The surgery is definitely recommended for dogs with a serious case of the disease.

Liver Shunts

A liver shunt is a birth defect that can be deadly. When a puppy is still in his mother's uterus, a vein carries his blood past his liver rather than circulating through it, since the puppy's mother's body filters all of the impurities out for her unborn puppies. Normally, this vein seals itself off, and the puppy's liver takes over its job at birth.

Sometimes, though, the vein remains intact. Instead of the puppy's blood getting cleansed and filtered in the liver, all of the waste products build up inside the puppy's system. In addition, the liver can't do its job of storing nutrients, so the dog won't have the necessary materials to build his reserves of energy and to help him grow.

Signs

The toxins in a dog affected with this condition can cause very serious neurological problems, including unconsciousness and seizures. Dogs with liver shunts often have digestive troubles, such as chronic diarrhea, and also may be unusually thirsty. Small size and failure to gain weight are very common in Yorkies with liver shunts.

Treatment

If you suspect a problem may be present, talk with your veterinarian right away. She will run some blood tests that will indicate if a shunt is a possibility. If preliminary findings indicate your dog may have a shunt, your veterinarian (or a specialist your veterinarian may recommend) will do further tests with equipment such as an ultrasound, CT scan, or MRI to determine the exact nature of your dog's problem. With this information, your veterinarian can recommend the best course of action for treating your dog's particular situation.

Depending on the severity of the shunt, your veterinarian might recommend managing the disease with medications and a low-protein diet. Some cases are best treated with surgery to close the shunt. Sometimes, the outcome is very good, and the dog will live a long life, but unfortunately, sometimes treatment will not be successful.

Liver shunts are considered to be hereditary, so it matters where you buy your Yorkie. If you buy a dog from a reputable breeder who is aware of the problem in the breed and only breeds healthy dogs from healthy stock, the chances of your puppy being healthy are good. If you buy from someone who doesn't know—or doesn't care—about the disease, the chances of having a sick puppy are high.

Be aware that one sign of a liver shunt is a dog who doesn't grow. That adorable, tiny "teacup" Yorkie just might be a very sick little puppy. Choose your breeder and your puppy carefully!

Pancreatitis

Pancreatitis is an inflammation of the pancreas. While any dog can get pancreatitis, Yorkies have more of a propensity for the disease than many other breeds. It is usually triggered when a dog eats foods that are high in fat, such as greasy table scraps. This is why you should be very careful about what you feed your Yorkie. One of the biggest days of the year at veterinary emergency clinics is Thanksgiving, because turkey (with skin), gravy, and all those other trimmings are high in fat. Your dog's little system most likely can't handle that kind of food.

Signs

Pancreatitis is a very serious, even life-threatening disease. Mortality is upward of 20 to 25 percent. Your dog may show signs of abdominal pain, loss of appetite, lethargy, depression, vomiting, and diarrhea. If you see these signs, especially if your dog has eaten some high-fat food, call a veterinarian immediately.

Treatment

Pancreatitis is treated with a stay at your veterinary hospital. The dog's digestive tract needs complete rest. He'll be put on an IV to receive fluids, and he won't receive food or water by mouth for a few days. Over the course of the next few days, your veterinarian will offer him small amounts of water and then food. Once he can drink and eat without causing a flare-up, he'll be allowed to come home. Your veterinarian will give you strict guidelines for what your Yorkie can eat, because once a dog has had an attack of pancreatitis, it is likely to recur if you aren't very careful.

Progressive Retinal Atrophy

Progressive retinal atrophy (called PRA) is a disease that causes blindness in dogs. Yorkies have a higher-than-average rate of later-onset PRA, which usually happens after about age seven. This is a hereditary disease, and all dogs who are going to be bred should be screened for the disease to make it less likely that their puppies will develop it.

Why Does It Cost More to Have My Yorkie's Teeth Cleaned Than Mine?

It can be frustrating to realize that you've just spent more money for your Yorkie's annual dental bill than you did for your own. The truth is that it is more labor intensive to clean your dog's tiny teeth than your own pearly whites.

The biggest difference is that dogs are put under general anesthesia when their teeth are cleaned. Veterinarians scrape and clean very aggressively to remove all the plaque, including probing around each tooth beneath the gum line. These are big instruments for a little Yorkie mouth, so your dog never could be comfortable having his mouth thoroughly cleaned without anesthesia.

If your dog is suffering from hypoglycemia, you may notice him seeming depressed or lethargic.

Signs

Vision loss with PRA is gradual. It often starts with difficulty seeing at night, so your Yorkie might bump into things on his evening walk. He may have trouble navigating from light to dark places. He may have trouble climbing the stairs or jumping on places he used to hop up on. If he seems to worry about going places or bumps into things, it may be because he's having trouble seeing.

Treatment

Unfortunately, no treatment for PRA is available at this time. Your dog will gradually lose his eyesight. The good news is that your Yorkie is likely to adjust very well to a lack of sight and enjoy himself just as much as he did when he could see.

While PRA is not treatable, responsible breeders can do much to prevent it. This is a hereditary condition, so if dogs with the disease aren't bred, the disease can be eliminated from the gene pool. The best defense against this disease is to only get a puppy from a breeder who has her dogs screened for PRA by a CERF (Canine Eye Registry Foundation) test. In this test, a veterinary ophthalmologist will examine the parents' eyes, looking for early signs of the disease. This exam should be repeated on all breeding stock every year.

There is hope that a genetic test for the disease will be developed in the future. Once a genetic test exists, then all carriers of the disease can be screened. Until then, the best way to prevent the disease from cropping up in the next generation is the CERF test.

HEALTH PROBLEMS COMMON IN TOY DOGS

Because of their small size, toy dogs have several conditions that every Yorkie owner should be on the lookout for.

Broken Bones

Little dogs have little bones, and little bones are breakable. This problem is compounded by the fact that Yorkies are energetic, fearless little guys who love to play.

Don't let your Yorkshire Terrier fling himself off tables or off the back of the couch, especially is he is a puppy or a fine-boned, little dog. Be careful when you pick him up, too; hold him carefully so he doesn't wriggle loose.

Signs

If your Yorkie is limping or yelping in pain, don't take a "wait and see" approach. While your dog might simply have sprained a toe or is showing symptoms of a chronic condition that isn't an emergency, you don't want to delay treatment if it really is a broken bone. Call your veterinarian (or emergency clinic if it's off hours) and tell them the symptoms you are seeing. If it appears to the veterinary office that your dog has a broken bone, they'll want you to come in right away.

Treatment

Treatment for your Yorkie's broken leg will be much like it would be for a human's. The first step is an x-ray. Treatment varies widely, depending on what bone is broken and the nature of the break. For a hairline fracture, your dog may just require rest. Other fractures may require a hard or soft cast. Some broken bones may require pins to keep the bone together while it heals.

Recovery time will be anything from a few weeks to several weeks, depending on the injury.

Dental Problems

Dental problems are common in all small breeds. If you think about it for a moment, it makes sense. A millimeter pocket in the gum of a human or a Labrador Retriever is a small problem. In a tiny Yorkie mouth, that pocket might lead to an extraction. Dental hygiene isn't just cosmetic. An accumulation of tartar, and

the resulting bacteria in the mouth, contributes to other health problems, including heart, liver, and kidney disease.

Preventive Care

Be sure to brush your Yorkie's teeth regularly. (See Chapter 5 for teeth brushing tips.) You also can do other things to prevent the accumulation of tartar. One of the best is to give your dog toys, such as stuffed animals, that naturally scrub his teeth when he plays. Let your Yorkie fetch his toy, and play a miniature game of tug-of-war with him. You'll both have a lot of fun, and you'll be flossing his teeth as you go.

In addition, give your Yorkshire Terrier chew toys for him to gnaw on. Nylabone makes chews that are suitable for Yorkies. Raw bones are also a good way for your dog to clean his teeth. Be sure that the bones are large enough so that he can't swallow them, and only let him chew bones while you supervise. Do not ever give your dog a cooked bone. A cooked bone will splinter and can cause internal bleeding.

Proponents of raw diets are emphatic that the enzymes in raw food help keep the teeth clean. If you're already inclined to try raw food, this is another fringe benefit. Otherwise, be sure your dog eats dry kibble, which can have something of a scrubbing effect on his teeth. Canned food is the worst choice from a dental perspective, and dogs fed only canned food tend to have a rapid accumulation of tartar and need more veterinary dental visits.

Signs of Dental Disease

Your dog's teeth should be bright and white, so any signs of yellow tartar should be discussed with your veterinarian. Also, if your Yorkie has "dog breath," it may be a sign of dental disease. Don't just accept the condition or try to mask it with doggie mints—go to your veterinarian for help.

Treatment: Going to the Doggy Dentist

Make sure that your veterinarian checks your Yorkie's mouth at least once a year. It is common for Yorkies to need annual teeth cleaning from a veterinarian. If you see tartar accumulation, or if your Yorkie is experiencing doggy breath, don't delay treatment. It only will make the problem worse.

For routine cleaning, your veterinarian probably will do a

good job. She may have a certified veterinary technician do the cleaning, or the veterinarian may do this. If the dental work is more complicated, though, it's a good idea to ask for a referral to a board-certified veterinary dental specialist. These veterinarians receive extra training and have more experience with dental problems. Procedures such as root canals, for example, are usually performed by a specialist. Sometimes tooth extraction in toy breeds can be tricky. They have tiny jaws that easily can break if a root is deeply embedded. If you have any doubt about whether the procedure your dog needs may be risky, ask for a referral to a veterinary dentist.

Like humans, dogs grow a set of "baby teeth" that fall out and are replaced by permanent teeth. By about six months of age, your Yorkie will have his adult teeth. However, small dogs tend to retain one or more puppy teeth, and Yorkies are no exception. If the puppy tooth hasn't come out on its own by the time the dog is about six to eight months old, it should be extracted, because it can cause adult teeth to become crooked (and add to dental problems in the long term). Some people wait until their puppy is about six months old to have him neutered, so that any extra baby teeth can be extracted at that time.

Hypoglycemia

Hypoglycemia, or low blood sugar, is most common in puppies between 6 and 12 weeks of age. This condition is one reason why most reputable breeders won't allow you to take a Yorkie puppy home before he is 12 weeks old. The vast majority outgrow the condition by the time they are seven months old, although some Yorkies must cope with the problem throughout their lives, especially if they are smaller dogs.

If you suspect your Yorkie is suffering from an ear or eye infection, take him to the veterinarian immediately.

Signs

A hypoglycemic episode is most likely to happen if your Yorkie is feeling stressed, has skipped a meal or has a poor diet, is cold, or has used up too much energy playing too long at one time.

You might notice your dog staggering, seeming depressed or lethargic, or acting disoriented. The condition also can cause your dog to slip into a coma and die.

Treatment

If your dog is showing signs of hypoglycemia, rub corn syrup or honey on his gums, or mix a little bit of the syrup or honey in some water and place it on his tongue. Meanwhile, call your veterinarian right away for instructions for further treatment. Repeated episodes can lead to more severe complications, so work with your veterinarian to manage this problem.

Yorkie puppies typically eat four meals a day until they are 12 weeks old, then three meals until they are 6 months old, and two meals during their adult years. If you have a dog who is prone to hypoglycemia, talk with your veterinarian about giving him more frequent, small meals to keep his blood sugar levels more even.

Luxating Patella

The kneecap in your dog's rear leg is attached by a groove in the bone. Because a Yorkie has tiny bones, it can be easy for the kneecap to pop out. This slipping of the kneecap is a common problem in all toy breeds, and the condition can range from a slight "trick knee" that won't affect your dog's quality of life to a serious, painful condition requiring skilled surgery.

A lot of controversy surrounds the issue of just how inheritable luxating patellas are. It is a very good idea to purchase your puppy from someone who has her breeding stock checked by a veterinarian for this condition before breeding her dogs.

Signs

With a luxating patella, watch for signs of limping or hopping involving your dog's rear legs. Dogs with luxating patellas often look like they're skipping, which seems cute until you realize it's the sign of what can be a serious medical condition. Veterinarians rate luxating patellas on a scale of 1 to 4, with 1 being a patella that can be pushed out of place but isn't painful, and 4 being a patella that is always out of place and very painful.

Treatment

Surgery is usually recommended for grades 3 and 4. Surgery is expensive and is usually performed by an orthopedic surgeon. Dogs with grades 1 and 2 are not normally in any pain, so they generally are watched carefully for symptoms. Depending on your dog's symptoms, your veterinarian might suggest that these dogs refrain from some activities, such as a lot of jumping.

OTHER HEALTH ISSUES

Yorkies don't have a high rate of diseases such as cancer or heart conditions compared with many other breeds. Still, all breeds face some common illnesses, especially in their older years, which you'll want to watch for.

Cancer

Dogs, like humans, are prone to cancer, especially in their older years. Cancer is the most common cause of death in older dogs. Happily, the treatment of cancer in dogs is rapidly progressing. Don't assume that a diagnosis of cancer is a death sentence. Chances are, it's not.

Signs

Look for obvious signs on your Yorkie. If you see a lump or bump, ask your veterinarian to take a look. Watch for sores on your dog's skin. Cancer often can have subtle symptoms, so look for the veterinary acronym "ADR"—short for "Ain't Doing Right." If your dog seems lethargic or just "off," take him to the veterinarian for a checkup.

Your veterinarian will

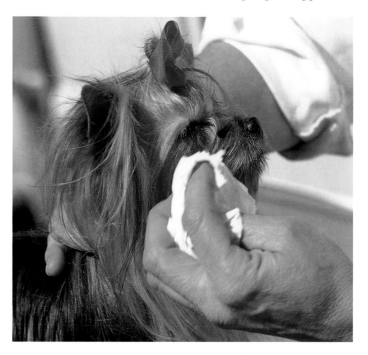

You can help prevent eye infections by adhering to good grooming practices.

Eye Infections

Yorkies have hair that can fall into their eyes, so it's important to be on the lookout for any signs of problems in your dog's eyes.

Signs

If your dog is squinting or pawing at his eyes, take him to the veterinarian to find out why his eyes are hurting him. Yellowish or greenish discharge from your dog's eyes is a possible sign of infection, and he needs to be seen by a veterinarian. If the whites of your dog's eyes are red, it can be a sign of an eye infection, injury, or allergy.

Treatment

The treatment that your veterinarian prescribes will depend on the diagnosis, of course. You may need to give your dog eye medication, and he may need to wear an Elizabethan collar (one of those gizmos that look kind of like a lampshade around your dog's neck) to stop him from scratching at or injuring the eye. Follow the veterinarian's advice to the letter, or you may have to start treatment all over again when the eye doesn't heal properly.

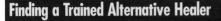

Finding a Trained Alternative Healer

Alternative medicine, like any other form of medicine, is best done by a trained professional. If your veterinarian is up on the latest technology, it is also possible that she is practicing alternative treatments such as acupuncture or chiropractic or can refer you to someone who is.

Here are some other places to find knowledgeable practitioners:

- **The American Holistic Veterinary Association (www.ahvma.org).** This association's website has a good discussion of alternative therapies and has a listing of members by state.

- **The International Veterinary Acupuncture Society (www.ivas.org).** This organization provides training and certification for veterinarians. Their website includes a listing of certified members. (You may also consider checking with a human acupuncturist in your area if your state medical and veterinary laws allow acupuncturists to treat animals.)

- **The American Veterinary Chiropractic Association (www.animalchiropractic.org).** This association provides training and certification for chiropractors and veterinarians. It has a list of certified practitioners on its website, which are split fairly evenly between the two professions. Members are from the United States, Canada, Europe, and Australia.

- **The Academy of Veterinary Homeopathy (www.theavh.org).** This organization trains and certifies veterinary homeopaths and lists practitioners on its website.

- **Linda Tellington-Jones (www.tteam-ttouch.com).** Her website gives a listing of TTouch practitioners around the world.

Heart Disease

Heart disease is common in older dogs, just as it is in people. Happily, treatment is available for heart problems. Many dogs, even with severe heart disease, live happy and fulfilling lives for many years.

Signs

Symptoms that might suggest a heart problem include difficulty breathing, tiring after physical activity, or a swollen belly. At your dog's annual physical, your veterinarian will listen to your dog's heart, checking for signs of disease such as a heart murmur, sounds of congestion, or odd heart rhythms.

Treatment

Treatment for canine coronary disease is almost identical to human treatment. It can range from medication, such as diuretics (to reduce fluid buildup), all the way to open-heart surgery and pacemakers.

As is true with any disease, take this one step at a time with your veterinarian. Find out the diagnosis, and then ask about treatment and prognosis. Your veterinarian might refer you to a veterinary cardiologist for the latest or most technical treatment options.

GIVING MEDICINE

One of the struggles that every dog lover faces is giving her dog medicine. This is usually a much bigger problem with small breeds than large breeds. If you have a Labrador Retriever, you can slip an enormous pill into a hot dog, and the dog is likely to swallow the whole thing, licking his lips in appreciation. On the other hand, your Yorkie is likely to notice a pill the size of a grain of sand in even the finest liver pate.

While you always can try hiding pills in your dog's food, the danger is that a sick dog will become very suspicious of what you're feeding him when he finds a pill in his food. Some sick dogs who already weren't eating well actually may stop eating because they are leery of the food.

Teach "Medicine"

If you have a finicky pooch, then, or if you're going to need to give your dog medication over a long period, teach him the word "medicine." First, you should calmly hold your dog. Have a favorite treat on hand; you might even want to show your dog the yummy treat that is waiting for him. Say, "Medicine," and quickly and efficiently give him the pill or liquid medication. Even if he squirms and wiggles, tell him, "Good medicine!" and instantly give the treat.

If you do this consistently for your dog, he'll learn to stand quietly and calmly take even distasteful medication—and then wag his tail, waiting for his reward.

When Your Dog Won't Swallow Pills

It can be hard to get a small dog to swallow a big pill. If you're having trouble getting pills down your dog's throat, ask your veterinarian if a liquid form of the medicine is available. If you have a small dog, it's easy to hold him with one hand and insert the liquid medicine through a syringe with the other.

If the veterinarian prescribes medication that requires large-sized pills or large amounts of liquid medication, ask her if an effective prescription is available that might fit better with a dog with a tummy the size of a golf ball.

If all else fails, you can carry out the traditional method of taking a pill and placing it as far back in the throat as possible, then gently stroking his throat until he swallows. Still, it's always better if you can give your dog medication with as little trauma as possible.

ALTERNATIVE AND HOLISTIC CARE

In the last decade, human medical science has acknowledged the value of many kinds of alternative care. Veterinary medicine has followed suit, and acupuncture, chiropractic treatments, herbs, homeopathy, and other alternative treatments are increasingly available for your Yorkie. These alternative treatments have lots of applications. For example, acupuncture can increase blood circulation, which might help a mild case of Legg-Calve-Perthes disease. Liver problems are common in Yorkies, and herbs such as milk thistle can sometimes alleviate problems.

There are times when Western medicine is best. If your dog has a broken bone, it doesn't do any good to give him herbs. For a

Proper Use of Alternative Medicine

Alternative care can benefit your dog in a variety of ways, but it should not be considered a replacement for veterinary medicine. If you are interested in alternative and holistic care for your dog, use it in conjunction with, not instead of, Western medicine.

If your dog ingests something you suspect may be poisonous, get help immediately.

urinary tract infection, a quick regimen of antibiotics usually does the trick. On the other hand, there are times when Western medicine doesn't have the best answer. Times also arise when a combination can help, too. For example, acupuncture or massage after surgery might help the healing process in some cases.

Some of the most popular alternative therapies are discussed in the following sections.

Acupuncture

When acupuncture is performed, hair-thin needles are gently inserted into the dog's skin. A skilled acupuncturist does not hurt a dog when she inserts the needles. Unlike hypodermic needles, which are designed to pierce tissue to deliver a shot, the thin acupuncture needles are designed to go between layers of skin. Acupuncture can help many conditions, including pain, allergies, and circulation.

Chinese Herbs

Chinese herbal medicine has been practiced for thousands of years, and practitioners of this modality think of Western medicine as being new and experimental! Chinese herbs can help treat many illnesses and in some cases may prove to be more effective than Western medications. Be sure that you are working with a skilled veterinarian (or the person prescribing the herbs is working closely with your veterinarian), because some herbs can interact with some medications. Don't treat your Yorkie with herbs that you get from the Internet or that just seem like a good idea. Herbs are just as powerful as other medicines, and using the wrong herb in the wrong situation can be a serious risk for your little dog.

Chiropractic Treatments

Doctors of chiropractic and trained veterinarians realign your dog's skeletal system so that it returns to healthy, functioning order. This can be very helpful after sports injuries (which little dogs can get as well as big dogs), accidents, and other events that put your Yorkie's body out of alignment. The American Veterinary Chiropractic Association provides training for chiropractors and veterinarians; the chiropractors learn about animal anatomy, and the veterinarians learn chiropractic techniques.

Homeopathy

Homeopathy is very popular today as a way to heal both humans and animals. First developed in the 1800s, the basic concept is that "like cures like." The idea is that a tiny dose of a substance can cure someone, while a larger dose will make the symptoms worse. Much like a vaccine teaches the body to have an immune response to a disease by introducing a debilitated virus, homeopathy is designed to help the body overcome an illness by introducing a small dose of a substance that also helps the body's system learn to counteract the problem.

Tellington Touch (TTouch)

This is a system of feather-like touch that relaxes and calms a dog. It also can help you establish a closer rapport with your pet. TTouch gives your pet a sense of well-being and may help him feel better if he's sick. Many TTouch practitioners teach classes, meaning that you can learn to TTouch your own dog. Several books and videos are available, many of which are carried at local libraries.

MEDICAL EMERGENCIES

Medical emergencies can happen at any time. If you think ahead and are prepared, it might make the difference between life and death for your little dog.

The following are some things to keep in mind:

• *Keep your veterinarian's phone number someplace handy.* If your dog is bleeding, you don't want to be thumbing through the phone book. Keep the number near the phone or taped to the refrigerator.

- *Know your emergency clinic.* In most larger cities and many smaller ones, after-hours emergencies are handled at special emergency clinics. Keep the number and directions to the clinic next to your personal veterinarian's information. If the clinic isn't on one of your regular routes, take the time now to familiarize yourself with how to get there, so that it isn't a worry if your Yorkie is sick.
- *Keep a first-aid kit on hand.* You can purchase a pet first-aid kit at pet supply stores or over the Internet, or you can put one together yourself. (See box.)
- *Purchase a pet first-aid book* (several good ones are on the market) and read it before a medical emergency arises, so that you'll at least know where to look if you need it. Keep your first-aid book with your first-aid kit.

Determining a Medical Emergency

Contact your veterinarian (or an emergency clinic) immediately if your Yorkie:

- has difficulty breathing
- is bleeding
- has a seizure

First-Aid Kit

The following are some items for your Yorkie's first-aid kit that will come in handy should an emergency arise:

- A muzzle (or soft cloth to make into a muzzle—all dogs can panic when they are in pain, and you don't want your Yorkie's fearful biting to get in the way of giving him emergency care)
- A "space" blanket that insulates against heat and cold
- Nonstick gauze pads
- Vet wrap (widely available—this is bandaging that sticks to itself).
- Towels (to wrap your dog in if he is cold or in shock, and to help clean dirt or blood)
- Antibiotic ointment
- Corn syrup (for treatment of hypoglycemia)
- Scissors

- Tweezers
- A syringe (no needle attached) to administer medicine or liquids
- Hot/cold pack
- Benadryl (in case of bee sting or similar incident—check for the dosage for your Yorkie with your veterinarian when you put the kit together, keeping a note of it with your kit)
- The number for your veterinarian and the nearest emergency clinic, and the address and directions to the clinic
- A pet first-aid book

In case of a natural disaster, make sure you have a safe place to take your dog.

- is acutely lethargic (can't move or stand up, seems unaware of his surroundings)
- has blood in his urine of feces
- has persistent, repeated vomiting—or persistently tries to vomit
- strains to potty
- can't move his legs
- has been hit by a car, even if he seems okay
- has an eye injury
- ADR—veterinary lingo for "Ain't Doing Right." You know your animal better than anyone else. If your gut tells you something is wrong, it is better to follow your instinct than to regret it later.

Foods, Drinks, and Drugs That Kill

Dogs and humans usually have a lot in common, and they often enjoy the same foods. However, a few snacks, drinks, and pills that won't hurt a human could prove fatal to your little Yorkie. Avoid them at all times!

Caffeine and Alcohol

An overdose of caffeine can cause your dog's heart to race, and too much even can cause cardiac arrest. Alcohol poisoning can kill

Pet Health Insurance

Several companies now offer health insurance for dogs. It can be a good option for Yorkies, especially because a variety of health problems in the breed (such as liver shunts, Legg-Calve-Perthes disease, and luxating patellas) can be expensive to treat.

Look for a veterinary health insurance company that has been around at least a few years. A number of companies have come and gone quickly in the last few years, and you want to be involved with one that's likely to still be around when you need it.

Be most concerned with the coverage of expensive items—routine care isn't what will make you choose between your mortgage payment and your Yorkie's medical care. Major surgery can put you in that position. It's a good idea to narrow your choices down to two or three companies and call them up. Ask them to tell you how much they would pay in a couple of scenarios, such as if your dog needed to have surgery for a luxating patella or if you needed hundreds of dollars worth of medication every month to treat a chronic disease. Pet health insurance only covers a percentage of the cost of care, so see if the numbers add up for you.

Alternatives to pet health insurance are available. Some veterinary clinics offer access to a company that provides loans to people who have pet health care costs they can't pay. You also might keep a credit card open with a high limit, just in case your dog needs it. Interestingly, more and more companies are offering pet health insurance as a company benefit. Take advantage of it if it is offered to you.

Figure out what makes sense for your home and your finances. It is a hard subject to tackle, but it's worth it to be a wise consumer.

a dog—and a little dog doesn't have to drink much to be at a toxic level.

Chocolate

Chocolate, even in small quantities, can be lethal to your Yorkie. Dark chocolate is more dangerous than sweet chocolate, but call your veterinarian if your dog has eaten any type of chocolate.

Cooked Bones

Never feed your dog a bone that has been cooked; raw bones may be okay with supervision. Cooking a bone, even briefly, causes the bone to become brittle, and it will break into sharp splinters when your dog swallows a piece. A cooked chicken bone is easy for a Yorkie to swallow and can become a medical emergency. Raw bones generally don't crack like cooked ones, and can be a safe treat if you supervise the dog. Of course, if meat is attached to the bone, be sure the dog chews it fairly quickly—you don't want the dog eating meat that has been sitting out for a long period of time.

Greasy, Fatty Foods

Yorkies are one of the breeds prone to pancreatitis; a fatty snack could send them to an emergency clinic.

Pain Medication—Including Ibuprofen

One regular-strength (200 mg) ibuprofen tablet can cause stomach ulcers in a 10-pound (4.5 kg) dog. Do not give your Yorkie aspirin or any brand-name pain reliever without discussing it with your veterinarian first.

Raisins, Grapes, and Onions

Recent studies have shown that raisins and grapes—even those that have been raised organically and have no pesticides—can cause kidney failure in dogs. Onions cause anemia. Other fruits and vegetables, though, are usually good treats.

Uncooked Bread Dough

The yeast in a dog's tummy can become a deadly brew. Uncooked bread dough ferments and turns into alcohol in a dog's system, which can poison your Yorkie.

CARING FOR YOUR SENIOR YORKIE

Just as humans lead more active, interesting lives longer than ever before, so do our dogs. Your Yorkie probably will be a healthy dog right into his teen years. The average Yorkie lives about 12 to 15 years, but many lucky owners have enjoyed their little dogs for 16, 17, and 18 years, and sometimes even longer.

The best way to help your dog live a long life is to be aware of senior medical issues, and work with your veterinarian to identify any problems early. At about age 8 or 9, it's time to talk with your veterinarian about your Yorkie's senior years.

The following are a few things your veterinarian might mention to you in the interest of maintaining your senior Yorkie's health.

Twice Annual Visits

Your veterinarian might suggest that your dog come in for exams twice a year instead of once a year. This is a good way to make sure that she is catching any problems before they become serious.

Blood Tests

Your doctor might suggest an annual senior blood workup to look for common problems in older dogs.

193

Canine Cognitive Dysfunction

This disease is much like Alzheimer's disease in people. Signs of canine cognitive dysfunction can include pacing, panting, getting lost in a corner of the house, and loss of potty training.

Just as humans are less likely to suffer from the symptoms of Alzheimer's disease if they practice mental and physical exercise, your Yorkie will be less likely to have cognitive problems if he remains active. Remember to give your dog exercise and play time, and keep teaching him tricks and games. (The expression "You can't teach an old dog new tricks" was written about people, not dogs!)

If your Yorkie develops canine cognitive dysfunction, your veterinarian can prescribe medications that can help him significantly.

Incontinence

While some housetraining problems are a symptom of canine cognitive dysfunction, they also can be a sign of some treatable bladder problems. Older female dogs, especially, can begin to have trouble controlling their bladders. Medication is available that is very effective in treating this problem.

Hospice and Palliative Care

Dogs of any age can develop terminal illnesses, or illnesses for which treatment may be more burdensome than seems right for that particular animal. If your dog is chronically ill, options other than euthanasia are available. With today's modern pain medications (and alternative treatments such as acupuncture), many pets can live comfortably for weeks, months, or even years with chronic conditions that otherwise would be intolerable. Even a terminal diagnosis doesn't mean that you have to put your dog to sleep right away. With pain management, you can spend the time saying goodbye and deciding how and when to let your dog go.

SAYING GOODBYE

You don't have to read this section while you're dreaming of getting a new puppy or are working on being the best possible owner for your Yorkie. But know that this section is here when you need it, and consider it advice from a friend to help you through a difficult time.

The life of every dog ends all too soon, even if you're lucky

Senior Needs

As your Yorkie ages, many aspects of his lifestyle likely will have to change. He may need to visit the vet for checkups more frequently, his diet and exercise routines may change, and he will be susceptible to new potential health problems. However, with the proper care, a senior Yorkie still can have many good years ahead of him as a part of your family.

enough to have your Yorkie well into his teens. The final gift you can give to your Yorkshire Terrier is to help him gently from this world.

When is it time to let go? People will try to give you a formula, such as "when the bad days outnumber the good ones, it's time to say goodbye." The reality of life, though, is that there isn't a numerical formula you can apply. No one knows your dog as well as you do, and he will let you know when he's ready to go. There are countless stories of people whose dogs gave them what seemed to be tangible signs of saying goodbye. A dog will pick up a toy he hasn't played with since he was a puppy and bring it to you, or he will go up to each member of the household with a special greeting. You can just feel it when a dog has closed the circle of his life. More likely, you will simply see the readiness in your dog's sweet eyes. He has lost his zest for life, his body hurts all the time, and he isn't interested in eating any more.

Your healthy Yorkie likely will live into his teen years.

A Gentle Procedure

Some dogs die naturally in their sleep. In most cases, however, they are ready to go before their bodies give out entirely, and it is a kind and loving act to end their suffering.

When your veterinarian euthanizes your pet, it is a painless, gentle procedure. Your veterinarian will simply give your dog a shot with an overdose of anesthetic. Your dog will softly fall into unconsciousness. When he is fully under the anesthesia, his heart will simply stop beating. It is quick and surprisingly peaceful.

It will help both you and your dog if you can be there for the

procedure. When you see the peacefulness with which your dog's spirit left this world, you will be comforted. It is also nice for your dog to have your loving presence with him as he gently falls into unconsciousness.

Mobile Veterinarians—an In-Home Option

Many communities have mobile veterinary clinics that will come to your home to euthanize your dog. For many people, it is comforting to have the dog on their lap on the couch or sitting outside with them in the sun when they say goodbye.

Whether it is a mobile veterinarian or your personal veterinarian who has cared for your dog for years, you will see the compassion and love the people in this profession have for the animals they serve. You will find the veterinarian kind to you and your dog and compassionate for you both.

Other Pets

Animals who share a home love each other as much as they love us. It is very helpful for them to see their buddy's body and understand that he is gone. "Animals understand death, but they don't understand disappearance," one of my wisest friends once said. So, if it is possible, let your other dogs (and cats if they were close to the dog) sniff his body. Let them understand what happened. Dogs who have seen the body of their friend are much less likely to frantically search for their missing companion.

Memorials and Rituals

Different people find different things helpful in the grieving process. No right or wrong answer exists—do what feels natural and right for you. To some people, an animal's body isn't important, and they would rather not have remains. Others find saying goodbye in a physical way helpful.

Burial

Many people find it a comfort to bury their little dog in a favorite place in the yard. Do be aware that some cities prohibit this, however.

Cremation

Cremation has become very common. You can scatter your

Yorkie's ashes in his favorite place to play. Alternatively, you can keep the remains in an urn, perhaps decorated with your dog's collar. You even can order artwork and jewelry that will incorporate some of your dog's ashes in the art.

Memorializing Your Yorkie

You may find countless ways to memorialize what your dog gave to you in his lifetime. Give a donation to an animal shelter or Yorkie rescue in your dog's name. Plant a tree. Write a poem. Do whatever brings you comfort. There is no "right" or "wrong" way to grieve a pet.

Pet Loss Support

The little dog with bright eyes and a loving heart changed your life. It is normal and healthy to grieve that loss. If you think some support would help you, ask your veterinarian if a pet loss support group exists in your area—many communities have them. The website www.petloss.com also has excellent resources that can help you work through your grief and come to a place where you can remember your life with your sweet dog with undiluted joy.

A LIFETIME OF GOOD HEALTH

It's scary to read about the things that can go wrong with your little dog's health. Remember, though, that most Yorkies live healthy, long lives. With all the love and care you're giving to your dog, he's likely to live an especially long and good life. Use the information in this chapter to help your little dog live that good life; don't let it upset or overwhelm you.

There is a magical relationship between dogs and people. Studies have proven that people experience lower blood pressure when they have a dog in the house. Guess what? Dogs have lower blood pressure when they're being petted by their human! So give your Yorkie a hug and enjoy each other every single day. You'll both be healthier—and certainly happier—for it.

RESOURCES

ASSOCIATIONS AND ORGANIZATIONS

Clubs and Registries

American Kennel Club (AKC)
5580 Centerview Drive
Raleigh, NC 27606
Telephone: (919) 233-9767
Fax: (919) 233-3627
E-mail: info@akc.org
www.akc.org

Canadian Kennel Club (CKC)
89 Skyway Avenue, Suite 100
Etobicoke, Ontario M9W 6R4
Telephone: (416) 675-5511
Fax: (416) 675-6506
E-mail: information@ckc.ca
www.ckc.ca

The Kennel Club
1 Clarges Street
London
W1J 8AB
Telephone: 0870 606 6750
Fax: 0207 518 1058
www.the-kennel-club.org.uk

United Kennel Club (UKC)
100 E. Kilgore Road
Kalamazoo, MI 49002-5584
Telephone: (269) 343-9020
Fax: (269) 343-7037
E-mail: pbickell@ukcdogs.com
www.ukcdogs.com

Yorkshire Terrier Club of America (YTCA)
Secretary: La Donna Reno
www.ytca.org

Rescue Organizations and Animal Welfare Groups

American Humane Association (AHA)
63 Inverness Drive East
Englewood, CO 80112
Telephone: (303) 792-9900
Fax: 792-5333
www.americanhumane.org

American Society for the Prevention of Cruelty to Animals (ASPCA)
424 E. 92nd Street
New York, NY 10128-6804
Telephone: (212) 876-7700
www.aspca.org

Royal Society for the Prevention of Cruelty to Animals (RSPCA)
Telephone: 0870 3335 999
Fax: 0870 7530 284
www.rspca.org.uk

The Humane Society of the United States (HSUS)
2100 L Street, NW
Washington DC 20037
Telephone: (202) 452-1100
www.hsus.org

Yorkshire Terrier Rescue Network, Inc.
President: Janine Huber
www.yorkshireterrierrescue.net

Sports

International Agility Link (IAL)
Global Administrator: Steve Drinkwater
E-mail: yunde@powerup.au
www.agilityclick.com/~ial

North American Flyball Association (NAFA)
1400 West Devon Avenue #512
Chicago, IL 60660
Telephone: (800) 318-6312
Fax: (800) 318-6318
www.flyball.org

Veterinary Resources

Academy of Veterinary Homeopathy (AVH)
P.O. Box 9280
Wilmington, DE 19809
Telephone: (866) 652-1590
Fax: (866) 652-1590
E-mail: office@TheAVH.org
www.theavh.org

American Academy of Veterinary Acupuncture (AAVA)
100 Roscommon Drive, Suite 320
Middletown, CT 06457
Telephone: (860) 635-6300
Fax: (860) 635-6400
E-mail: office@aava.org
www.aava.org

American Animal Hospital Association (AAHA)
P.O. Box 150899
Denver, CO 80215-0899
Telephone: (303) 986-2800
Fax: (303) 986-1700
E-mail: info@aahanet.org
www.aahanet.org/index.cfm

American Holistic Veterinary Medical Association (AHVMA)
2218 Old Emmorton Road
Bel Air, MD 21015
Telephone: (410) 569-0795
Fax: (410) 569-2346
E-mail: office@ahvma.org
www.ahvma.org

American Veterinary Medical Association (AVMA)
1931 North Meacham Road – Suite 100
Schaumburg, IL 60173
Telephone: (847) 925-8070
Fax: (847) 925-1329
E-mail: avmainfo@avma.org
www.avma.org

British Veterinary Association (BVA)
7 Mansfield Street
London
W1G 9NQ
Telephone: 020 7636 6541
Fax: 020 7436 2970
E-mail: bvahq@bva.co.uk
www.bva.co.uk

Miscellaneous

Association of Pet Dog Trainers (APDT)
150 Executive Center Drive Box 35
Greenville, SC 29615
Telephone: (800) PET-DOGS
Fax: (864) 331-0767
E-mail: information@apdt.com
www.apdt.com

Delta Society
875 124th Ave NE, Suite 101
Bellevue, WA 98005
Telephone: (425) 226-7357
Fax: (425) 235-1076
E-mail: info@deltasociety.org
www.deltasociety.org

Therapy Dogs International (TDI)
88 Bartley Road
Flanders, NJ 07836
Telephone: (973) 252-9800
Fax: (973) 252-7171
E-mail: tdi@gti.net
www.tdi-dog.org

PUBLICATIONS

Books

Lane, Dick, and Neil Ewart. *A-Z of Dog Diseases & Health Problems.* New York: Howell Books, 1997.

Rubenstein, Eliza, and Shari Kalina. *The Adoption Option: Choosing and Raising the Shelter Dog for You.* New York: Howell Books, 1996.

Serpell, James. *The Domestic Dog: Its Evolution, Behaviour and Interactions with People.* Cambridge: Cambridge University Press, 1995.

Magazines

AKC *Family Dog*
American Kennel Club
260 Madison Avenue
New York, NY 10016
Telephone: (800) 490-5675
E-mail: familydog@akc.org
www.akc.org/pubs/familydog

AKC *Gazette*
American Kennel Club
260 Madison Avenue
New York, NY 10016
Telephone: (800) 533-7323
E-mail: gazette@akc.org
www.akc.org/pubs/gazette

Dog & Kennel
Pet Publishing, Inc.
7-L Dundas Circle
Greensboro, NC 27407
Telephone: (336) 292-4272
Fax: (336) 292-4272
E-mail: info@petpublishing.com
www.dogandkennel.com

Dog Fancy
Subscription Department
P.O. Box 53264
Boulder, CO 80322-3264
Telephone: (800) 365-4421
E-mail: barkback@dogfancy.com
www.dogfancy.com

Dogs Monthly
Ascot House
High Street, Ascot,
Berkshire SL5 7JG
United Kingdom
Telephone: 0870 730 8433
Fax: 0870 730 8431
E-mail: admin@rtc-associates.freeserve.co.uk
www.corsini.co.uk/dogsmonthly

WEBSITES

Dog-Play
www.dog-play.com/ethics.html
A cornucopia of information and pertinent links on responsible dog breeding.

The Dog Speaks
www.thedogspeaks.com
Canine behaviorist Deb Duncan's site, filled with useful advice on canine etiquette, behavior problems, communication, and relevant links.

Petfinder
www.petfinder.org
Search shelters and rescue groups for adoptable pets.

Boldfaced numbers indicate illustrations.

A

AAFCO (Association of American Feed Control Officials), 71
accidents, housetraining, 102, 105, 106–107
acquiring a Yorkie. *See also* breeders; selection and suitability
    adoptions, 40–42
    puppy selection, 43–46
acupuncture, 188
adoptions, 40–42
adult dogs
    diet and feeding, 67
    housetraining, 105
    vs. puppies, 30–31
aggression
    in multiple-dog households, 47
    towards dogs, 26, 131–133
    towards people, 133–136
    warning signs of, 129
agility competitions, 144, 146–147
air travel, 60
AKC. *See* American Kennel Club
alcoholic beverages, 77, 191–192
allergies, prescription diets for, 76
alternative therapies, 185, 187–189
American Kennel Club (AKC)
    breeder profiles, 37–38
    Canine Good Citizen (CGC) test, 139–140
    founding and activities, 8
    registration procedure, 48–49
    shows, 141
anesthesia, 171
animal-assisted therapy, 150–151
Animal Poison Control Center, 77
animal welfare groups, 198
antifreeze, 58
appearance, 15–20, 44–45
ASPCA Animal Poison Control Center, 77
Association of American Feed Control Officials (AAFCO), 71
associations, 198
avocados, 77

B

baby gates, **50**, 54–55
bad breath, 95, 180
barking, 22, 129–131
    debarking surgery for, 132
basic commands. *See* commands, basic
bathing, 89–91, **91**
bed privileges, 102, 135–136
behavior. *See also* temperament
    breed traits, 20–21, 97–98
    dog body language, 129
    human leadership and, 100–101
    socialization and, 97–98
behaviorists, 133
behavior problems, 128–137
    aggression towards dogs, 26, 131–133
    barking, 129–131
    getting help with, 133
    growling or snapping, 133–136
    housetraining accidents, 106–107
    toy possessiveness, 128, 136–137
Best in Show, 142–143
Best of Breed, 142–143
birds, **26**, 27
boarding kennels, 61
body, breed standards, 16
body language, 129
body parts, teaching names of, 84–85
bonding, 58–59, 100–102, 125
bones, feeding of, 76–77, 192
books, 200
bowls, food and water, 52
bread dough, 78, 193

breeders, 32–40
    criteria for, 33–37
    documents from, 46–51
    importance of, 32–33
    selection of, 37–39
    unethical, signs of, 35–37
    visits to, 39–40, 42
breed history, 5–13
    in England, 6–10
    father of breed, 9–10
    Scottish origins, 5–6
    in United States, 10–13
breeding Yorkies, 170–171
breed standards, 15–16
Britain. *See* England
broken bones, 179
brushing, 87–89, **89**
burial, 196
buying your Yorkie, 43–46. *See also* breeders; selection and suitability

C

caffeine, 191–192
cancer, 183–184
canine cognitive dysfunction, 194
Canine Eye Registry Foundation (CERF), 35
canine freestyle, 150
Canine Good Citizen (CGC), 139–140
canned food, 72–73
carriers, for air travel, 60
car travel, 59–60, 110
castration, 31, 171–173
catch, 116–117
cats, 27
celebrity Yorkies, 12, 13
CERF (Canine Eye Registry Foundation), 35
CGC (Canine Good Citizen), 139–140
characteristics, 15–27
    appearance, 15–20
    breed standards, 15–16
    child interactions, 23–25
    companionability, 21–22
    dog interactions, 25–27
    exercise needs, 20, 22–23

ABOUT THE AUTHOR

Deborah Wood is the award-winning pet columnist for *The Oregonian* newspaper and the author of several pet books, including *A New Owner's Guide to Papillons* and *Little Dogs: Training Your Pint-Sized Companion*. She lives with three Papillons and a cat in Portland, Oregon. Deborah competes with all of her Papillons in obedience trials and makes regular animal-assisted therapy visits with one of her dogs to a children's hospital.

PHOTO CREDITS

Photo on p. 12 courtesy of Losevsky Pavel (Shutterstock)
Photo on p. 21, 79, 153, 197 courtesy of WizData, Inc. (Shutterstock)
Photo on p. 78 courtesy of Paulette Braun
Photo on p. 104 courtesy of Lisa F. Young (Shutterstock)
All other photos courtesy of Isabelle Francais and TFH archives

Nylabone® Cares.

Millions of dogs of all ages, breeds, and sizes have enjoyed our world-famous chew bones—but we're not just bones! Nylabone®, the leader in responsible animal care for over 50 years, devotes the same care and attention to our many other award-winning, high-quality, innovative products. Your dog will love them — and so will you!

Toys   Treats   Chews   Crates   Grooming